Crosspaths in Literary
Theory and Criticism

Italy and the United States

RENEWALS 458-4574

DATE DUE

GAYLORD			PRINTED IN U.S.A.

Gregory L. Lucente

CROSSPATHS IN LITERARY THEORY AND CRITICISM

Italy and the United States

STANFORD UNIVERSITY PRESS
STANFORD, CALIFORNIA   1997

Stanford University Press
Stanford, California
© 1997 by the Board of Trustees of the
Leland Stanford Junior University
Printed in the United States of America

CIP data appear at the end of the book

Stanford University Press publications are
distributed exclusively by Stanford
University Press within the United States,
Canada, Mexico, and Central America;
they are distributed exclusively by
Cambridge University Press throughout
the rest of the world.

For Gloria

Preface

THE GOAL OF THE following essays is to trace the development of several of the most important recent trends in both the American and the Italian critical traditions, with occasional exploration of the points at which these two traditions intersect or for specific reasons fail to intersect. Throughout, the primary focus is on literary questions, but attention is also given to the broader concerns of culture as a whole and, when relevant, to economic, social, and political phenomena. While analysis of the form of discourse plays a part in many of these essays, the aim of the individual pieces as well as of the collection in its entirety is to come to terms not just with the formal organization of literary and critical discourse but also with the underlying generative principles from which form results, which is to say with ideology.

The collection is divided into three parts. Part I is made up of essays on recent theoretical trends, including deconstruction, Marxism, and feminism; critical pluralism; the history of Marxist critique; and certain problems within cultural studies. In each piece in this section, the major emphasis is placed on American theoretical developments, with a secondary emphasis on markedly differing elements of the Italian tradition. The contrasting of American and Italian views here brings the characteristics of each into clearer relief and at the same time provides a critique of these positions.

The essays in Part II analyze historical imagination as expressed in literary and sociohistorical criticism. The first three essays of this section treat Italian writers who have discussed these topics on a theoretical level, principally Giambattista Vico and Antonio Gramsci; the fourth takes up the turn to both history *and* myth in Luigi Pirandello's last plays; and the fifth examines the literary depiction of social life in the "historical" novels of Elsa Morante, William Faulkner, and Mario Vargas Llosa. All of these essays begin by considering social history and historical representation as evidenced in highly influential works of literature and theory, works that both reflect and re-create the driving concerns of European, American, and Latin American society of their own time and of the time of their historical frames. The basic intent of this section is to make explicit the fundamental historical-theoretical perspectives of the collection overall.

Part III treats three literary debates and opens with two essays on primarily American topics. The essays in this section focus first on the reaction in the United States to the discovery of the wartime writings of Paul de Man and second on the "against theory" debate. Finally, the study's conclusion sets forth a model of cultural analysis that seeks to avoid the mystifications of Gianni Vattimo's *pensiero debole* ("weak thought") *and* the reductive drawbacks of traditional Marxist views of literary production and expression (both American and Italian) while taking advantage of current, more ample materialist perspectives arising out of gender studies in the United States. A further concern here is to delineate the differing characteristics and goals of modernism and postmodernism in the light of the ongoing discussions of this question, with an eye to bringing the entire collection up to date.

In sum, even though the collection's interests are preponderantly American, the essays overall are intended to demonstrate the utility of Italian views as critical correctives. The constant concern is thus to develop a historically attentive evaluation of literature and culture that sees literary/cultural phenomena not as mere reflections of socioeconomic forces but as formative components of social life in the contemporary intellectual environments of both Italy and the United States.

Earlier versions (1983–89) of chapters 5, 6, 7, and 8 have been published in English and of chapters, 1, 2, 3, and 11 in Italian. The journals of original publication are *New Vico Studies, Forum Italicum, Spunti e ricerche, L'ombra d'Argo, Lettere Italiane*, and *Allegoria*. The remaining chapters (4, 9, 10, 12) appear for the first time in the present volume.

This study has been a long while in the making, and I would like to thank at least a few of the people who have helped along the way: Eduardo González, John Irwin, Paolo Volponi, Timothy Bahti, Tobin Siebers, Alina Clej, James Porter, Giovanni Cecchetti, Jonathan Culler, Stuart McDougal, Giuliana Minghelli, Romano Luperini, Franco Fortini, Henry Remak, Giorgio Tagliacozzo, Craig Frisch, Deanna Shemek, Giuseppe Mazzotta, and Robert Dombroski. My greatest debt of gratitude is owed to Gloria Lauri Lucente, *sine qua non*.

G.L.L.

Contents

xii   *Contents*

PART ONE

RECENT THEORY

1

Deconstruction, Marxism, and Feminism in Current Theory

Representation and Totality

IN ONE WAY OR ANOTHER, American literary theory of the last twenty-five years or so has characteristically dealt with a pair of intertwined concerns: on the one hand the question — or, perhaps better, the problematic — of representation, and on the other the question of totalities. While it is true that the three dominant trends in critical theory in the United States over this period, that is, deconstruction, Marxism, and feminism, approach these two topics in notably different ways, it is also the case that a review of these very differences tells us something about both the trends under consideration and the underlying questions themselves. The aim of such an exercise in comparison of theoretical approaches, then, is not so much to establish the limits of the varying positions in the manner of an overview or a survey, but rather to suggest possible means to cast beyond their limits. As is perhaps not surprising given the declared sociohistorical interests of recent American critical thought, including that of cultural studies, one of these means will turn out to be not only aesthetic or even literary/critical in its orientation but social and, in a quite specific sense as regards developments in "postmodern" Italy as well as in the United States, political.

Before suggesting what I mean in this sphere by "political," or more precisely political engagement, it might be best to take up, one by one, the salient aspects of these three major trends both as historical moments and as ways of thinking. When deconstruction came to America around 1970, its attack on conceptual totalities of every stripe — be they ethical, political, religious, or whatever — as well as its relentless drive to locate and destabilize what had previously seemed stable oppositions — inside/outside, part/whole, and the like — gave deconstruction's discourse the aura and the attraction of both novelty and profundity. The novelty was due in large part to the basic ignorance of the American critical audience as regards the nineteenth-century German roots of much deconstructive thought, roots that include the work of Kant, Hegel, the early Marx, and Nietzsche and then lead up through Husserl to Heidegger and Freud. The aura of profundity deserves a somewhat more extensive explanation. True, the interest in both rhetoric and hermeneutics that informs so much work done in what we would regard today as a deconstructive mode seemed *a priori* to have a special sort of seriousness or depth, at least to an audience trained in the American secondary school system, in which philosophy as a subject is rarely taught except via literary texts, and in the American university, in which literature departments continued to be influenced by the New Critical distrust of any appeal to theory in the abstract, which is to say to any account of poetics or interpretation as something apart from close "practical" readings of literary works. But deconstruction's aura of profundity derives, it seems to me, from a further cause, too, as regards an American audience, and that cause has to do with deconstruction's fascination — one might almost say obsession — with language.

Although this fascination dovetailed in important ways with the preexistent interests of such New Critics as Warren, Brooks, Ransom, and others — interests deriving primarily from the concern for language in Renaissance and metaphysical poets as well as in Coleridge, Wordsworth, Keats, and the European romantics — it steered American criticism's perspective on language in a new direction, one growing out of European structuralist conceptions of linguistics as an object of study. To put it baldly, the usual deconstructive and poststructuralist view was that language, and by extension literary language, could be conceived of as a coded system of signifiers and signifieds in which linguistic meaning feeds back *not* into something outside of language (the everyday world of matter and sense, or, at the opposite extreme, transcendent metaphysical truth) but, rather, into language itself, albeit in the motion of continual deferral. This conception of language or "text" as the ground for truth — a ground that is, however, not thereby grounded — can be seen, *mutatis mutandis*, as constituting an organizational parallel to such competing systems of thought as traditional Marxism, in which meaning is seen to feed back into economic materialism and class struggle, and more recent feminism, in which meaning is seen to feed back into the problems of gender. But more significantly here, this tenet of deconstructive belief concerns interpretive totalities, and most importantly of all with regard to deconstruction's influence on critical theory in the United States, it concerns the very notion of representation. The underlying conceptual pairing of language and world, which deconstruction, in its assault on prior critical verities, did not really do away with so much as destabilize to the extent of privileging language over its previous "worldly" master, remained in critical discourse primarily as a sort of whipping boy, a *pharmakos* to be identified only in order to extricate its insidious results root and branch. The problem, of course, was that in the process representation, as a notion depending both on the unity of language and the world and on the immediate transparency of language in order to re-present the truth of the world, was conceived of as a totality, as a totalizing notion that deserved, again, not so much outright destruction as gradual, if not always subtle, deconstruction.

It is true that the destabilizing of the language/world pairing had varying effects in the writings of different practitioners of deconstructive criticism and theory. Derrida's delight in self-reflexive free play in the realm of the signifier, including puns, Freudian word games, and multilanguage jokes, is fairly obvious in his writing, as is de Man's elucidation of the entire category of the aesthetic, at times in the mode of almost ascetically demystifying rigor but at other times in the mode of *vertige* or even angst. But all in all, deconstruction's reaction against anything it construed to be a version of representational totalities remained consistent, and its critique consistently negative. This situation is not strange given that totalizing thought tends to proceed by uniting disparate entities and building them into established conceptual and perceptual wholes with an ultimate goal of harmony, whereas deconstructive thought typically proceeds by breaking down constructed concepts into their constituent parts and setting these parts, however they may be construed, to work with and against one another in a process of continuing destabilization. What *is* strange in relation both to seemingly unified totalities and to deconstructed conceptions is that in each type of thought the most significant aspects are often those that are either unidentified or, indeed, left out altogether. As will be detailed in the chapters that follow, totalizing thought, in contrast to its apparent program, often operates most successfully when it is based on prior and/or ongoing exclusions rather than inclusions, and deconstruction often operates by undermining unified authority in one area or field of examination only to reestablish authority, however surreptitiously, in contiguous realms.

What I have said so far as regards representation has had to do with representation as a literary or, more broadly speaking, an aesthetic category, but it also holds, with a few refinements to be noted shortly, for representation as a political category. Despite Derrida's often-expressed interest in the phenomena of politics, it is very difficult to see how the discourse of deconstruction, contrary as it is to any concept of representational commitment *or* stability, can play a genuine part in the discourse of practical politics, other than perhaps in the politics of egotism or anarchism. This is the case across the political spectrum, I believe, because politics, deconstruction's characteristic account of things notwithstanding, is not merely discursive but is instead always that *and* something more, whether that something more has to do with the everyday nonacademic world, with the commitment of belief and action, or with both of these. But I am getting ahead of the story in relation to the political, a topic treated from varying perspectives in the coming chapters. It would be more orderly at this juncture to point out a pair of difficulties to which deconstruction fell prey as it came to have an established role in the American critical enterprise in the 1970's and 1980's.

The first of these difficulties went along with the process of deconstruction's intellectual entrenchment in the American critical community, whereas the second derived not so much from deconstruction's intellectual content as from the effect of that content on its followers (and eventual adepts), which is to say from deconstruction's effect upon what can be termed, *grosso modo*, pedagogy. As regards the first issue, it is undeniable that deconstruction brought a breath of fresh air to an intellectual environment still dominated by the critical techniques and the critical presuppositions of New Critical and structuralist formalism (including not only formalist literary practices but also the New Critical moral/political beliefs as expressed in the essays of *I'll Take My Stand*). But it is also the case that the eventual entrenchment of deconstructive discourse in the American academy led, maybe inevitably, to a kind of stagnation, and in this instance a rather distinctive brand of intellectual stagnation, that of nihilism. More significant still is the effect that deconstruction had on its younger American enthusiasts. This effect is treated in some detail in the chapter on the discovery of the wartime writings of Paul de Man. Suffice it to say here that one of the more uncanny results of the establishment of deconstruction within the American university was the creation, simultaneous with the instituting of new models of interpretation, of a newly authoritative critical/theoretical voice in which to explicate and disseminate those models. The quality of this voice — polemical, self-assured, in short, intellectually totalizing — would not seem at all strange in the ambience of literary theory except for the fact that the usual deconstructionist practice (in the writings of de Man and Derrida but also in those of J. Hillis Miller, Geoffrey Hartman, Barbara Johnson, and many others) was to work against each and every form of totalizing conceptualization. In other words, it is not hard to see, along with the late Freud of *Beyond the Pleasure Principle*, that removing the pillars of stability in one sense led of necessity to their reestablishment in yet another sense. Undercutting any and all concepts of stable totality on the part of deconstructive thought thus often meant — in terms of deconstruction's reception by students, colleagues, readers, and so forth — the re-creation of stable authority on the part of deconstruction's ingeniously authoritative voice, which is to say, and here both Derrida and de Man are especially germane, the reception of the "voice of the master." With respect to totalization and authority, then, what deconstruction took away with one hand, it gave back with the other.

The Marxist discourse reintroduced into the American literary academy in the early 1970's exercised a dual attraction, by its wholeness and by its invitation to commitment. The "new" Marxist critics shared the banner of novelty with their Parisian structuralist (and later poststructuralist) confreres, but Marxism differed from the various forms of structuralist and poststructuralist criticism precisely in its aspirations, first, to create a totalizing form of social analysis and, second, to put that analysis directly into play within a broader social context. True, the standard Marxist analytical program aimed to unmask the ideologically motivated — thus obfuscating — totalities of bourgeois thought and thereby dismantle the edifice of mystification that simultaneously hid the true sources of sociopolitical meaning (the relation of classes to the economic modes of production and the class struggle itself) and perpetuated the dominance of the bourgeoisie. In this sense, then, the newer American Marxist critics (Fredric Jameson, Stanley Aronowitz, et al.) adopted a detotalizing analytical stance when they approached the cultural production of capitalism, hewing to reflection theory only to demonstrate the ways in which literature represented not some sort of timeless, ideal truth but instead the material situation of the artist, the work of art, and the audience in social life. Nonetheless, since the American Marxism of the 1970's and 1980's tended not only to decompose the totalities of previous bourgeois criticism but also to constitute a new set of totalities based on a materialist rather than an idealist model — no matter how pluralist or flexible the newer model may have appeared at first blush — the totalizing potentials of contemporary Marxism in

America remained effectively in force (one thinks, for example, of Jameson's work on Balzac or Myra Jehlen's on Faulkner).[1]

In spite of the initial attractiveness of recent Marxist criticism in the United States, however, both the aspiration to wholeness and that to commitment deserve to be considered, today, from a more critical vantage point. Each of these aspirations might be usefully considered in light of the work of Fredric Jameson (which is treated in more detail in the chapter on the history of Marxist criticism in the United States). In his writings up through *The Political Unconscious*, Jameson offers two sorts of critical approaches, on the one hand criticism of ideology (the literary work seen in its expressive relation to its own tradition and to its present) and on the other hand critical appeals to utopian thought (the work seen as a potential projection of future-oriented, postrevolutionary social desires and situations). What is important to see here is that Jameson thereby elides the fundamental moment of revolutionary transition.

This elision is especially telling in relation to another sort of totality, that is, the traditional Marxist assertion — in evidence at least since Lenin and Gramsci — of the necessary unity of theory and practice, about which Jameson's work cannot help but create a rather obvious doubt. In short, the suspicion is this: that American Marxist theory works exclusively because it is *divorced* from practice, because it has become, after 1970, nothing but an academic discourse. Marxist literary theory in the United States may thus be seen, in this light, as a totalizing discourse but *not* as a genuine totality, since the concrete social element of theoretical application is utterly foreign to both its authors and its audiences. The nexus of commitment and totality thus takes on a fairly strange cast, that of a sociopolitical theory that is committed to a position toward society and politics only as a theory, which is to say only across the protective, totalizing distance of academic abstraction and institutionalization.[2]

It is in this context of the academic institution that Jameson's slogan "Always historicize," stated at the outset of *The Political Unconscious* but implicit in much of his writing both before and after, should be examined. All in all, it seems that in the absence of any genuine notion of revolution, and in the absence of any actual arena for revolutionary praxis, the effect of such a slogan is to make each of these concepts — revolution *and* praxis — into historical entities and therefore into elements of our past, distanced and somehow assured, rather than of our present or future, pressing and engaged. This lack of a genuine sociopolitical program in the United States, indeed, of any notion of what a genuine program would entail, may well reflect the same uncertainties that beset the Communist Party in Italy (uncertainties so obvious in the recent dispute over the "crisis of the [party] name") and that helped to undo Marxist states in the Soviet Union and the entire eastern bloc. Such uncertainties indeed make Jameson's regular appeal to critical "shock" as a value in and of itself seem more akin to the theoretical positions of Barbara Johnson in her deconstructionist phase and even of Ezra Pound (i.e., "Make it new!") than to the principled positions of Gramsci and Adorno, not to mention Marx and Engels.[3] Although it may well be true that what is currently needed in the West as well as in the East is a completely new and different story — or representation — as to what revolution is all about, it seems unlikely that American Marxist criticism, with its sophisticated yet apolitical theoretical outlook, will be able to go very far in restructuring the total social world of any, or better, of anyone's, concrete future in either a representational or any other sense.

American feminism, as regards totalities and representation, has fared somewhat better. There are several concrete reasons why this is so, but before I mention them I would like to contrast Jameson's work with the recent work of an Italian/American feminist critic, Teresa de Lauretis's *Technologies of Gender*.[4] Like Jameson, de Lauretis has a characteristic opposition running throughout her works. But whereas his is between ideology and utopian projection, hers is between representation and politics, or more precisely representational strategies and political activity. De Lauretis is an especially appropriate writer in this context owing to the pointed similarities and contrasts that can be drawn between her work and Jameson's, but many other feminist writers could be adduced, too.

For example, in Judith Butler and Joan Scott's widely discussed anthology treating feminist theory and politics, just about every author deals with the topics that de Lauretis discusses with greatest emphasis: foundations as opposed to contingencies, idealist thought as opposed to political praxis, utopian goals as opposed to more limited legal and sociocultural aims (abortion rights, sexual harassment, physical violation, discrimination in the workplace and the marketplace, and sociocultural issues of power, gender, and class).[5]

Since both Jameson and de Lauretis claim—and I believe justly so—a materialist bias, it may well seem, at least at the outset, that the distinctions to be drawn from these differing pairs are mere quibbling. But the implications of these differences should not be taken lightly. To fill in just what these implications are, a further point should be made: for American feminist critics of the last twenty years or so, "political activity" has meant fighting not only for equality but also for one primary right, that to control the material destiny of women's own bodies (with a secondary emphasis, it is true, on lesbian rights). The struggle for legalized abortion has kept a good number of those critics interested in feminist topics intimately involved in both social protest and political/judicial action, and this despite the fact that many in the United States either thought or hoped that the entire matter had been settled, even if only in its broad outlines, by the Supreme Court decision in Roe versus Wade. At any rate, regardless of all initial expectations, the abortion issue in the United States—which has been revived by recent court decisions and legislative activity at local, state, and national levels—has turned into the controversy that will not go away, and in the course of this unpleasant transformation it has kept feminist critics politically active in a direct and tangible manner.

Thus, in contrast to their Marxist colleagues, American feminist critics have not had the luxury of adopting either the politically abstract posture of practical indifference or the politically disengaged one of "wait and see." There is simply too much immediately and urgently at stake in the ongoing disputes over abortion, sexual harassment, and sexual violence—much more than there is in any generalized discussion, within a materially comfortable society like the United States, of economic or even moral injustice. To put this in other terms, over the past twenty-five years or so, while American Marxist criticism has turned into a strictly academic undertaking, American feminist criticism has become materialism not only for the press and the classroom but also for the courts, the legislatures, and the streets. This situation has been affected as well by the tenure system of the American university. Although it is true that Marxist academic *writing*, at least academic writing narrowly defined, has not carried an especially strong taint even in the post-McCarthy period, Marxist political *action* on the part of younger, untenured American professors does in fact carry a stigma within the academy (as I discuss further in Chapter 3), especially within the more conservative sectors of the humanities such as English departments. However, partially because of political traditions and partially because of academic prejudice (or, in this instance, the felicitous lack of it), academic activists involved in feminist causes, tenured or untenured, do not suffer at present as great a stigma. Hence it is much more likely that a young American feminist critic will feel free both to write in an engaged way *and* to act in the service of his or her beliefs than will a more traditional Marxist critic to do so.

Recent feminist criticism in the United States has been shaped by other issues as well. One of these is the dispute over essentialist as opposed to contingent conceptions of the so-called social "construction" and the social functioning of gender. This dispute has been influenced by English and French feminism but is also very active within American feminist criticism itself (one thinks here again of the various positions treated in the work of de Lauretis, or in the incisive writings of Sherry Ortner on the relations between gender, patriarchy, and capitalism). Also of concern to American feminists are the questions of theoretical sophistication and political involvement discussed in so many of the studies devoted to openly contrasting American and French feminism. In such discussions, the usual characterization of these two differing "schools" makes the French seem quite sophisticated indeed and the Americans considerably more practical, in terms of both everyday politics and ho-hum, step-by-step empirical analysis (though, once more, it may seem that in this sphere, too, the sum exacted for obsessive theoretical sophistication is paid precisely in political estrangement and uncertainty). It would be nice at this point to be able to clarify such distinctions through appeal to an Italian model or even a series of models, and there actually is an up-to-date and informative book on Italian feminism by Lucia Birnbaum.[6] Unfortunately, however, Birnbaum's book demonstrates the paucity of original feminist thought in Italy, at least in Italian academic circles, with the single exception of the social sciences. (Whether such paucity springs from the traditionally patriarchal influence of the Church, from the usual difficulty of the Marxist left in treating the status of women and other gender questions *as* questions of gender, or from the masculine-oriented hierarchy of the Italian academic institution itself, Birnbaum does not attempt to say.)[7]

But of all such questions, the most apropos here brings us back to the problems of totalities and representation. Whereas the typical procedure of deconstructive discourse, as we have seen, was to break apart totalities while actively replacing them with *voice*, recent American feminism, owing in part to such influential French writers as Monique Wittig, has tended to avoid the totalizing effects of impersonal theoretical discourse precisely through consistent, at times adamant, personalization of the critical voice. Nevertheless, despite this tendency, there remains a problem, which to my mind is one of the more nagging and even debilitating features of a good deal of feminist critical conceptualization: the personalization of the speaking *subject* of representational discourse, perhaps because of the very value that the exclusive category of "the personal" thereby acquires, may go hand in hand with the universalization of the represented *object* of criticism, at least insofar as that object is constituted by discourse's "other," in this case what has become known as "the white Western male" of feminist criticism (who knows who he is or where he lives). In this process, the crucial distinctions among men — biological, social, cultural, economic, and political — often get pushed aside in order to keep feminism's discursive train on track, with a concomitant gain of personalized energy and innovation and a concomitant loss of conceptual validity. In other words, it seems that the authentic advances of feminist criticism within the realm of materialist sociocultural analysis have on occasion been limited, and I think unnecessarily so, by that criticism's difficulty in conceiving of the "other" of its world in ways that go beyond monolithic terms — oddly enough, the very monolithic terms of bourgeois capitalism — and this is true not only of the world such criticism describes but also of that which, willy-nilly, it enters.

As is most likely clear from what I have said up to now, it does not seem to me that these limitations are either desirable or inevitable. This is why, irrespective of the innovative and timely contributions of recent feminist thought in the struggle to free theoretical discourse from the tyranny of the totalizing "objective" voice of patriarchal capitalism, I would prefer a field of investigation conceptualized not so much as "feminist studies" than as what is often termed "gender studies," that is to say, an area of materialist thought in which men and women are equally capable of participating so that the "objective" accident of biology, whether in a Freudian sense or any other, is in point of fact *not* destiny.

Here I would like to turn briefly to the debate over the distinctions between modernism and postmodernism as it occurs in a series of current critical studies in both the United States and Europe. A relatively direct path to this topic passes through the work of Terry Eagleton, at times carried forth *solus ad solam*, at times in dialogue with Fredric Jameson.[8] Disagreeing fundamentally with Jürgen Habermas, both Eagleton and Jameson, as well as Gianni Vattimo (to be discussed shortly), believe that such a phenomenon as postmodernism really *does* exist. That is to say, again in opposition to Habermas, they believe that the project of modernism, with its emphasis on individual dissolution and alienation as well as its constant attempt to reestablish the lost ground of interpretative authority and closure, has come to an end socially as well as culturally. For Eagleton, the distinctive characteristic of postmodern society is the very pervasiveness of culture itself, embellished by postmodernism's delight in interminable self-reflection and pastiche as well as by its invitation to collective immersion in the re-creative activity of cultural production and enjoyment. There is no doubt that Eagleton perceives the potential danger of such phenomena, that he understands all too well that the joy of antielitist collective delight runs perilously close to the narcissistic involution of individual hedonism and consumption and that the production of postmodern culture, while it may appear somehow autonomous, with an integrity all its own, is inextricably tied to the market situation of postmodern technological development and to the internationalization of the dominant world economic community. But, overall, Eagleton's handling of the entire question of postmodernism, with its new sense of the individual and the community as well as its new economy and culture, is notably evenhanded.

But so far, as Eagleton notes in various contexts, the same cannot be said for Jameson. Where Eagleton sees at least the potential for parody — and so for an ordered hierarchy of values even if in a self-reflective hall of mirrors — Jameson sees only pastiche, only the antihistorical enticements of solipsistic self-involvement with no hope of either rational order or effective escape. A part of this attitude derives, it seems to me, from the core of almost puritanical seriousness that can be found in much of Jameson's work. But still more to the point here is Jameson's dogged adherence to a version (however restructured and updated) of Lukácsian reflection theory, from which perspective this new culture is essentially a reflection of a new economic organization. Since that new economy remains tied to the same oppressive bourgeois forces that created and, at least in the final analysis, organized the culture of modernism under industrial and monopoly capitalism, the culture produced by the current international capitalism of "high tech" must be equally suspect: unquestionably a new band, but still the same old tune.

On the other hand, Vattimo, in his recent treatment of "The Transparent Society," is extraordinarily enthusiastic about pretty much everything that postmodernism, and especially what he terms postmodern "chaos," is up to. In a sense, this enthusiasm is, in and of itself, heartening. Nonetheless, Vattimo's work does create certain perplexities. One of these arises from his fleeting discussion of socioculture life in what he appears to regard as the postmodern society par excellence, the United States. Along with a philosophical overview of the sorts of issues we have mentioned so far — issues concerning the socioculture immersion of the individual/collective subject in the nonhierarchical and nonauthoritatively ordered, that is, postmodern, society — Vattimo offers an interesting perspective on human liberation and the freedom of the word, the very access to speech, in contemporary American life: "Negli Stati Uniti degli ultimi decenni hanno preso la parola minoranze di ogni genere, si sono presentate alla ribalta dell'opinione pubblica culture e sub-culture di ogni specie" ("In the last several decades in the United States, minorities of every sort have begun to speak out, groups and sub-cultures of every kind have taken the podium of public opinion").[9] True, Vattimo is quick to hedge his bets, to admit that perhaps it should be recalled that complete "political emancipation" has not actually gone along with this apparent liberation and that ultimate economic power still resides in the hands of the great corporations; and he is also critical of the very concept of transparency as regards contemporary society. But all in all, his depiction of American life, indeed his conception of postmodern culture and society in its totality, is nothing short of glowingly optimistic.

It would be nice to be able to share his optimism, but this is not possible. Certainly, the errors that Vattimo makes, at least by implication and suggestion, should be pointed out. In the first place, the two "major" American minorities among those that Vattimo alludes to, women and blacks, provide difficult examples at best, since women are once again assailed by the abortion issue, as mentioned above, and blacks have not had anything like the economic advancements in relation to whites that the liberal enthusiasts of the 1960's predicted for them. In the second place, any hint that subcultural groups are now speaking out in liberation and sociocultural affirmation seems misguided, even ridiculous, in the light of the highly publicized activities of those groups that at present come most quickly to mind, the symbol-defined yet also extraordinarily violent gangs engaged in bloody internecine warfare in the black and ethnic neighborhoods of Los Angeles, New York, Chicago, Detroit, and other large American cities.

But my intent here is not to quarrel with Vattimo over the facts: that would be too easy. Instead, the question I propose at this juncture has less to do with the details of what Vattimo says than with why in the world he would want to say it. The answer seems all too obvious. Vattimo's conception of life in the United States, indeed his entire notion of "the transparent society" toward which we all should strive, remains functionally fixed in the totalizing optimism of its conception of the world, that is, its representation of the world, only to the degree that it actively ignores and/or glosses over the biting material facts of that world. It should perhaps not surprise us then that Vattimo's view of America corresponds remarkably well with George Bush's announced desire for a "kinder, gentler America," a type of society in which contrasts exist but do not dominate, in which difference is itself happily transparent, in which the sociocultural experience of each subject is at once authentically individual *and* authentically collective: in short, the society of postmodernism. As I say, all this should not surprise us. But it should disturb us.

Why? For the simple reason that if we, too, are taken in either by Vattimo's re-creative representation of contemporary life or by that of politicians like Bush, in a sort of fantasy that recalls not the everyday world around us but rather the world of Snow White and the Seven Dwarfs (and here the allusion to Hollywood is not in any way gratuitous), we will lose whatever genuine choice we have in actually *participating* in both sociocultural and political life, that is, in the realities of our own world. In my opinion, Jameson's view of postmodernism is too negative, and it may well lead to a sort of nonparticipation by abstention. But Vattimo's view is far too positive, and in the end considerably more dangerous, because it may well lead to nonparticipation by default, by giving up our real ability to choose and negate — in short, to cut back the sociopolitical bushes of current American life if not to uproot them completely, as they perhaps deserve. Although when all is said and done I am not against theory (à la Knapp and Michaels or anyone else), I am against theorizing for its own sake, against the sort of theorizing that seems to move only in circular fashion as a protective justification for its own continuing discourse (in this instance, à la Vattimo), blissfully apart from the actual particulars of the world of its creation and reception. It seems to me finally regrettable that so much of the writing on postmodernism, carried out from so many different perspectives, turns out to be of this stripe.

To conclude, I would like to make three proposals. All of them entail a new sense of commitment on the part of both the writers and the readers of literary theory. The first of these proposals is that we refresh our notion of theory as something that must be grounded in *and* tested against texts, literary, cultural, critical, and theoretical. The second is that we renew our notion of sociocultural *commentary*, which must be not only culturally informed but also socially engaged in a direct and meaningful way. The third proposal, which is perhaps even more pressing in the United States than in Italy, is that we revitalize the program for political action in order to move the academy, along with its constituent members, to where it should be — and where, at certain times in American life, like the 1930's and 1960's, it has been — in direct contestation of the political elite. Although Edward Said's notion of contrastive criticism in comparative literature is helpful in all these areas, I do not believe it takes us far enough in the direction of understanding our relation to either society or politics, because theory's goal is, or should be, not just to get inside of them — where it is of necessity anyway — but also to find ways to get outside of them, in the key not of acceptance or even of retooling but of genuine choice and change.[10] At any rate, all three of these points will come up again in the course of the following chapters. Here, it will suffice to repeat Fredric Jameson's historicist call to arms of the 1980's: "Always historicize!"[11] But for god's sake, don't stop there.

2

Critical Pluralism in the American and European Traditions

The Advantages and Disadvantages of Pluralist Interpretation

E pluribus unum

CRITICAL PLURALISM, the simultaneous adoption of multiple critical approaches to literary texts, is an established fact of both literary criticism and literary pedagogy in the United States. Indeed, it has become one of the more salient features of American critical discourse in the "postdeconstructionist" era, as is evidenced by the attention it has drawn in *Critical Inquiry* and other major journals.[1] Although American pluralism has a recognizable institutional center, the University of Chicago, and an at least roughly discernible group of major practitioners, including such figures as Wayne Booth, Stanley Fish, E. D. Hirsch, and Fredric Jameson (each of whom will be discussed here), pluralism's influence in American critical discourse is so widespread that it cannot be easily delimited. Part of the reason for this pervasiveness is that pluralism in America has roots that extend well beyond literary studies as such, and even beyond the humanities in general, to include the discourse and the practice of both economics and politics.

Once this broader historical perspective has been assumed, the differences between American critical pluralism and such recent European trends as Jacques Derrida's deconstruction and Gianni

Vattimo's *pensiero debole* ("weak thought") become considerably clearer. Prior to considering such differences, however, I will sketch out the similarities between these four American critics, similarities that are at times predictable and at times surprising. A necessary first question is: what are the general characteristics of American pluralism? As Ellen Rooney has argued in a brilliant, groundbreaking study to which I am greatly indebted, pluralism is a critical praxis that is both constituted and limited by what she terms "the problematic of general persuasion." As Rooney points out: "The pluralist may be a partisan of *any* faction in the critical field, from intentionalist to feminist, myth critic to Marxist, so long as [he or] she practices (and of course preaches) a contentious criticism founded on the theoretical possibility of universal or general persuasion."[2] This problematic requires that pluralist discourse imagine an intellectual environment in which, first, every individual critic or reader is subject to persuasion and, second, each instance of critical discourse aims to persuade all the individuals making up the community. In Rooney's terms, each critical utterance must work to persuade every reader. This program thus demonstrates not only the flexibility of pluralism's discourse but also its patently humanist slant.

Despite the obvious strengths of such a program, it should be noted from the outset that pluralism's problematic of general persuasion carries with it important drawbacks. Primary among these is the perhaps not astonishing fact that pluralism itself is unable, or at least unwilling, to name the problematic of general persuasion. I say perhaps not astonishing because pluralism is, as one of its foremost proponents claims, a "common-sense" practice, a nuts-and-bolts critical approach that tends to eschew abstract self-reflection and concentrate instead on concrete particulars.[3] The pluralist operates *with* pluralism's problematic rather than thinking *about* it. Even when pluralists do step back to examine their critical practice, they concentrate on it as practice instead of examining its theoretical presuppositions, all of which means that pluralism never arrives at a clear consideration of its workings as a critical praxis or, more significantly here, as a worldview, which is to say, as an ideology.

At first glance, pluralism's characteristic blind spot may seem casual or coincidental, but on closer examination it becomes clear that pluralism's failure to acknowledge the ideological underpinnings of its program is far from unmotivated. This brings us to the second of pluralism's shortcomings, which turns out to be, regardless of the seeming inclusiveness of the problematic of general persuasion, the nature of pluralist exclusion. Pluralism has no rigorous concept of exclusion, even though every *critical* statement necessarily excludes some other sorts of statements and/or counterstatements. Exclusion, as a normative notion openly imported into pluralism's discourse, would create an unthinkable gap in the imagined continuity of the critical community — a continuity that is posited *a priori* by pluralism's problematic and that must be regularly reaffirmed if pluralism's practice is to succeed. Regardless of pluralism's ultimate fear of disagreement or of genuine, irremediable difference, however, pluralism does exclude, as Rooney quite convincingly asserts. Just what pluralism excludes is in fact exclusion; that is, in the "problematic of general persuasion, the absent or excluded term is exclusion itself."[4] Rooney reaches this conclusion following the work of the American political and intellectual historian Gary Wills, who in turn follows Louis Hartz (who, of course, follows Tocqueville) in Hartz's analysis of the dangers of "unanimity" in American democracy and his critique of the ahistorical myth of self-evidence that is endemic in American liberalism blissfully cut off from the class-related conflictual roots of the bourgeois struggle in Europe.[5]

What are some of the potentially exclusionist discourses that pluralism would exclude? A rigorous, strictly materialist Marxism is one, a thoroughgoing gender-determinant feminism is another. But any sort of exclusionist discourse qualifies — that is, qualifies to be excluded — ranging from traditional paleography, with its concern for the scholarly establishment of the text, to some (though not all) traditional exegesis, with its concern for *definite* levels of graded meanings, to historically oriented *rezeptiongeschichte*, with its concern for the *real* nature of historically verifiable audiences, to such more narrowly defined but equally steadfast approaches as the triangular theory of mimetic desire based on the functions of the scapegoat in the later work of René Girard or the archetypal criticism of the early Northrop Frye. In short, any discourse that attempts to forefront a univocal source of meaning is automatically barred from pluralism's supposedly universal universe. The critic must agree, as a requirement for entrance into the pluralist community, to be open to persuasion — that is, not to have an overriding bias. Any definitely committed criticism, criticism that shows its own interests and that is committed to anything other than the problematic of general persuasion, is thus left out. It is important to emphasize that this exclusion is a given of pluralistic discourse, since it is the set of *a priori* exclusions effected by the problematic of general persuasion that preserves the purity of the pluralist community within its (unseen, or better, unspoken) bounds and that thus gives pluralism's discourse the appearance of universality. In other words, while the pretense of pluralism is a *gradual* process of contention, consideration, and exclusion in order to get at the universally persuasive truth of things, the reality of pluralism is *de facto* exclusion operative from even before the very beginning.

Owing in part to the success (and resultant attention) that pluralism has enjoyed in American criticism and in American education, certain of pluralism's academic practitioners — indeed, certain of its champions — have recently begun to perceive the chinks in their armor and have, as is only natural, endeavored to fashion the appropriate repairs. First among these has been Wayne Booth, who has attempted to address not only the "powers" of pluralism but also its "limits."[6] Booth writes out of a long and distinguished tradition at the University of Chicago, which includes as its founding fathers Ronald Crane, Richard McKeon, and Elder Olson.[7] In turn, this tradition itself has roots in the broader realm of American pragmatist philosophy; and it is not merely fortuitous that Booth's standard opposition between pluralism and various forms of narrowly committed criticism, which he terms "monisms," shares the terminology adopted by William James in the Hibbert Lectures on "The Present Situation in Philosophy," delivered at Oxford in the spring of 1908 (though Booth makes it clear, invoking Crane, that James's "radical pluralism" is simply not radical enough).[8]

In spite of Booth's cavils, it is important to see the overall impact on American pluralist thought made by the sort of distinction that James drew in urging his pragmatist understanding of pluralist empiricism as "the habit of explaining wholes by parts," and in opposing any and all forms of monistic rationalism, or "the habit of explaining parts by wholes."[9] James's characteristic insistence on coming to terms with what he calls "the particulars of life" goes a long way toward explaining the intellectual background of the nonreflective discourse of pluralism, with its special silences, and it also suggests why Booth is at pains to assert that "common-sense untheoretical pluralism" is of such value — *nota bene*, such pragmatic value — because, when all is said and done, it "works."[10] In another context, moreover, Hugh Kenner has described the peculiarly American perspective of such writers as Hemingway, Faulkner, Fitzgerald, and Williams as sharing this same concern for empirical particularity, infused, to be sure, with symbolic power, in the sort of "homemade world" that distinguished the aesthetic climate and the aesthetic practices of early-twentieth-century American modernism.[11]

To return to Booth's defense of pluralism, it might be well to pass on to his attempt to deal specifically with the limits of pluralism in a forum bearing that phrase as a title (and including as well papers by M. H. Abrams and J. Hillis Miller), which was sponsored by the Modern Language Association's Division on Philosophical Approaches to Literature and subsequently published in *Critical Inquiry*. In this essay, Booth calls for a return to the balanced critical values of vitality, justice, and understanding, and he does so by way of appeal to criticism's sense of community, not only as a community of readers but also as one of other authors. As Booth says, "I would care even more . . . about whether the critic acknowledges community with the other *authors* he treats."[12] It is not difficult to see that this is another version of the pluralist community discussed earlier: everyone admitted must agree beforehand to try to persuade, to try to understand, to try to agree. In Booth's words:

"Nothing I have said or anyone can say about vitality makes any sense *unless we all believe* that people can understand each other, sometimes, and that they should *always try to* understand."[13] The ontological contingency of understanding ("sometimes") is countered by the absolute imperative of the willingness to understand ("always"), both of which, however, are of only secondary importance, since the primary epistemological requirement of the pluralism program remains in force without regard to temporal or ontological refinements: "unless we all believe." The totalizing power of this sort of argumentation permits Booth not only to admit that the limits of pluralism are themselves plural but also, in the end, to extend entry to the realm even to monists, as long as they will themselves agree to play by the pluralist rules; that is, as Booth says, "Give your neighbor's monism a fair shake."[14]

When in his early work Booth challenged the notion of the author and replaced it with the "implied author" inherent within the literary text, he did away with one sort of monistic interpretive procedure and opened the text to the sorts of multiple readings that are characteristic of pluralist discourse. When in his later work Booth encounters the problem of the absence not only of "the author" but also of authority, he reconstitutes the function of authority by recourse to the notion of community. Although this notion is treated in open fashion only briefly in Booth's work, it does provide a link, however tenuous at first, to the writings of another pluralist critic thoroughly steeped in the American tradition, the most adamant and consistent proponent of the interpretive force of communities, Stanley Fish.

Fish's work over the past several decades has been instrumental in displacing the meaning of literary texts from various traditional positions of determinate stability, first in Fish's concentration on the workings of both the literary construct of the reader and the text-centered "self-consuming" artistic artifact and then, as his theoretical position developed further in the direction of the emotional experience of reading, in "affective" stylistics. Each of these stages of development did away with traditional monistic models of interpretive authority, but without reconstituting authority in any stable fashion. In this sense, as well as in Fish's adherence to the problematic of general persuasion and to the exclusions regularly practiced by pluralist criticism, Fish's works recall those of Booth; but in attempting to reestablish the notion of authority within interpretive communities themselves, Fish's work goes considerably further than anything Booth has attempted.

In his later phase, Fish remains committed to the necessarily subjective and contingent nature of interpretation. He says in a polemical reply to objections to his position made by John Reichert: "When Reichert or anyone else identifies something — an object, a text, an intention — as being available independently of interpretation, I know in advance that it could not be so and I look immediately for ways to demystify or deconstruct it. I always succeed."[15] But even though the *objects* of perception depend on the *act* of perception for their meanings — and therefore, for Fish, on interpretation — this does not imply that such meanings are themselves utterly free or infinite. Meanings and interpretations depend on the community of perceivers. Whether the consensus of the community is conscious or unconscious, the meanings available to any object in the process of interpretation will be constrained by the authority of the communal understanding. The concept of the indeterminacy of meaning thus continues in force while at the same time limits are imposed, now in a "communally" (rather than an individually) subjective fashion.

This theoretical position could lead to practical consideration of various historical communities of readers, which is to say, in accord with the line of development of Fish's thought, from the notion of "the reader" to that of "readership." But in spite of occasional anecdotal examples of concrete incidents (culled mostly from Fish's personal experience in the classroom), there is little or no historical slant to Fish's work, which thus remains, regardless of its material/historical potentials, not only polemically subjectivist but also thoroughly idealist. While attempting to introduce a concept of communal controls for interpretation, Fish neglects to develop any mechanism for the implementation of such controls, and the result takes on the odd configuration of an interpretive community that consists in a single, stellar member, Stanley Fish. Fish's version of the communal authority of the hermeneutic circle thus appears more like that of a hermeneutic merry-go-round, one that is run by the individually authoritative professor himself.

There is a further aspect of Fish's thought that deserves consideration. This has to do with the idea of "theory." As we have noted previously, American pluralism, with its roots in pragmatism, is not generally given to self-critical theorizing. What *works* is what is valuable, and no amount of abstract, theoretical self-examination or self-awareness, divorced from critical practice, will ever add very much to whatever it is that we, as critics, know and do. Fish reaches a somewhat similar conclusion as regards critical theory and critical consciousness, yet he does so from a distinctly Fishian perspective. Since, according to Fish, everyone who is part of the community is *in* the community, there is no way for any member, including the critic, to get outside of the community. Theorizing, like any other practice, must therefore remain within the bounds that the community tacitly accepts, and this is the case whether such theoretical discourse is critically self-conscious or not.

In this respect, therefore, any distinction between theory and practice is bogus, since *all* sorts of thought and discourse are governed by the same kinds of communal rules. Practical criticism should thus not be threatened by theoretical discourse, any more than the reverse should be true, because theory itself, as a kind of bugbear menacing the communal calm from the darkness beyond, does not, and by definition *cannot,* exist. If this notion of interpretive limits sounds strangely deterministic coming from an apologist for the indeterminacy of meanings, so be it. Fish intends, however, not to annoy or upset his audience but — or at least so he claims — to console them. He explains this intent at the conclusion of the essay that provides *Is There a Text in This Class?* with its title:

Of course, solipsism and relativism are what [Fish's opponents] fear and what lead them to argue for the necessity of determinate meaning. But if, rather than acting on their own, interpreters act as extensions of an institutional community, solipsism and relativism are removed as fears because they are not possible modes of being. That is to say, the condition required for someone to be a solipsist or relativist, the condition of being independent of institutional assumptions and free to originate one's own purposes and goals, could never be realized, and therefore there is no point in trying to guard against it. [Fish's opponents] spend a great deal of time in a search for the ways to limit and constrain interpretation, but . . . what they are searching for is never not already found. In short, my message to them is finally not challenging, but consoling — not to worry.[16]

For Fish, the mere fact of being able to propose a theory or pose a question means already "having" an answer since to formulate the question means its answer is *already* available within the community. In another mode, a few pages later in the book, Fish repeats essentially the same message: "So it would seem, finally, that there are no moves that are not moves in the game, and this includes even the move by which one claims no longer to be a player. . . . What I have been saying is that whatever [critics] do, it will only be interpretation in another guise because, like it or not, interpretation is the only game in town."[17] And so, for Fish, the critic's egotistical boast, "I always succeed," is just part of a much larger and in the end a much more (self-servingly) satisfied dictate: business as usual.

In these and other instances, one of Fish's regularly specified opponents is E. D. Hirsch, the author of two influential books on literary interpretation and the best-known American advocate of authorial intention as the key to literary understanding.[18] Hirsch, in the view of Fish and many of his American confreres, is not a pluralist, since his intentionalist stance makes him appear to be a critical monist. But within Hirsch's work, authorial intention, or what Hirsch terms "meaning," is complemented by another object of critical inquiry, what he terms "significance," or, roughly speaking, the amalgam of contextual effects generated by and/or accruing to a literary work. Literary history, reader response (idealized or historically conceived), genre criticism — any objects of literary investigation not concerned with the intentions of the author — fall under the critical heading of significance and are thus fitting concerns for critical investigation.

By adding the critical category of significance to that of meaning, Hirsch broadens his horizons in pluralist fashion; but this is not the only sense in which Hirsch is, just below the surface, a pluralist. Indeed, Hirsch's conception of meaning as authorial intention is already a fuzzy, nonrigid sort of monism, one capable of giving over quite easily to pluralist discourse. This is true in part (leaving aside the question of whether meaning can *ever* be totally noncontextual) because of Hirsch's basic mistrust of the possibility of establishing authorial intention in any manner: "The fact that certainty is *always* unattainable is a limitation which interpretation shares with many other disciplines."[19] But this haziness is also the case owing to Hirsch's disinclination to create a full-fledged monism within the critical community: "The limitation of verbal meaning to what an author meant and the definition of understanding as the construction of that meaning does not . . . constitute a narrow and purist notion of meaning."[20]

Despite Fish's charges, Hirsch enters the pluralist kingdom not only because of his acquiescence to the problematic of general persuasion and his adherence to pluralist exclusion, but also because of his acceptance of simultaneously adopted multiple approaches to the work of art and his avoidance of what might have been, in other hands, a genuine critical monism. Although Hirsch has expanded on several of these issues in his subsequent work and has still more recently sketched the outlines of his developing opinions to be published in forthcoming books, his further efforts, as he himself admits, are merely refinements of his previous ones, not major changes or deviations. According to what he says in the 1986 issue of *Critical Inquiry* devoted to the topic "Pluralism and Its Discontents":

I would stress that the refinements I am currently making in the analysis of implication still operate under a communicative model of interpretation, whereby implications are governed by authorial intent. I regard the refinements as a technological advance, not a technological revolution. I shall not be offering a radically new Compact Disc player, but just a better phono-cartridge, arm, and turntable to play the same old record with greater fidelity.[21]

The inclusion of Hirsch in pluralism's arena should serve if nothing else to suggest the engulfing powers of pluralist ideology and pluralist discourse in American literary criticism. Nor is Hirsch the only "odd fellow" to finally take up residence within the bounds of the pluralist camp. Even such an apparently committed critic as

Fredric Jameson — whose battle cry "Always historicize!," whose repeated insistence on "History itself" as the undeniable grounds for interpretive truth, whose attentiveness to questions of ideology and to "the priority of the political interpretation of literary texts," and whose contention that "only Marxism" provides compelling and convincing answers to the problems of interpretation that he addresses should, taken all together, make him a genuine monist — turns out, in his own extraordinarily eclectic critical practice, to be a thoroughgoing pluralist in monist clothing.[22] Samuel Weber has suggested as much, and Ellen Rooney has been able to demonstrate Jameson's pluralism in some detail, despite his statements to the contrary; but Hayden White, who wrote the blurb for *The Political Unconscious* that was used by Cornell University Press, must already have had, knowingly or not, the same feeling when he warmly recommended the book to scholars across a wide variety of fields and when he praised Jameson for his simultaneous adoption of a large number of critical perspectives: "No one else encompasses as many positions within a disciplined critical practice."[23] But neither Jameson's idealist view of "history" (evidenced in part by his emphatic capitalization of the word, as Weber has pointed out) nor his extraordinary syncretist energies provide a full account of the pluralist cast of his work, which is due as well to the very vagueness of Jameson's concept of the "political." In Jameson's work, this category is not a unitary or pure one, like the relation between social class and the modes of production in classical Marxist thought, or like established political power and authority in more recent praxis philosophies; and it is indeed to a certain extent this very flexibility, this concept of the political as a broadly based, second-level sort of notion, one that includes, at times, culture, social organization, issues of community, and even the motivated representation of community, that lends Jameson's argument its richness and breadth. But it also opens the door to the pitfalls of pluralism, and this is so throughout *The Political Unconscious*, whether Jameson is examining textual surface or ideological underpinnings.

In the past few decades, moreover, pluralism's influence has managed to enter not only the discourse of obviously pluralist critics but that of their occasional opponents as well (the later work of M. H.

Abrams being perhaps the best example among a great many). The debates over feminism in recent American criticism have also been affected by the often unseen problematics and exclusions of pluralism. Even principled attempts to limit pluralism from inside its own borders, like that by Paul Armstrong in *PMLA*, in 1983, are really beside the point, since pluralism's most striking effect in American criticism is its external, all-encompassing force.[24] American pluralism, like a giant Pac-man set loose, thus gobbles up friends and foes alike and goes happily on its way.

It is time to ask why this should be the case. Part of the reason for pluralism's eminence in American critical discourse is undoubtedly historical. I have mentioned that contemporary critical pluralism has roots in the history of American philosophy, specifically in nineteenth-century pragmatism. (While I have stressed the influence of William James, Armstrong concentrates on that of C. S. Peirce; Booth would most likely add the more recent influence of John Dewey to the list.) But political, economic, and religious history are also relevant. The founding of the American state in the eighteenth century, with its Enlightenment influences of participatory democracy and deism, effectively bracketed the *source* of meaning — be that source immanent or transcendent — to privilege the inevitably multiple *effects* of opinion, belief, and interest, that is, of interpretive perspective, in everyday life. The doctrine of the separation of church and state in a nation constituted by a strong Protestant element, for which every reading of the sacred text was valid only in the relation between the individual and the deity without any need for the univocal word of the Church for affirmation, merely heightened the pluralist multiplicity already implicit in political democracy. These characteristics are especially notable when the contrast is drawn between the United States and the Continental traditions of France, Italy, and Spain (with a major pluralist exception embodied in Germany's Hans-Georg Gadamer). It is also of interest that one of the current spokesmen for pluralism *within* the Catholic tradition, David Tracy, is a theologian with a teaching position at the University of Chicago.[25] The economic underpinnings of American capitalism are equally germane. It is, of course, important to remember that "the business of

America is business" and that in the liberal bourgeois marketplace what works is, well, what works. But for the moment, in the context of interpretation and the literary text, it might be more useful to consider the effects of pluralism on the institution with which, as professional literary critics, we are most deeply involved, the American university.

It is not hard to see, along with Tocqueville and generations of social historians after him, that institutionalized democratic inclusion and freedom bring with them the often unacknowledged dark side of exclusion and tyranny; and it is instructive to transfer these notions back to the academy *as* an institution. The professionalization of literary studies in America after the Second World War — a process in which the business marketplace served not merely as an influence but, in many respects, as a model — occurred at roughly the same time that pluralism within literary criticism became the dominant factor. I am not going to dwell here on the issues at stake in the "loss" of traditional humanism in the contemporary academy or on those in the debate over "history" and "theory," but will focus instead on a topic that has to do with both of these questions, the definition of and attitude toward comparative literature in today's academic climate. Even though pluralist critics have often used the topic of pedagogy as a field of pragmatic consideration to further their views (and Booth, at least, has broadened his horizon to include both literary pedagogy and university politics), comparative literature as such has rarely if ever received contemporary pluralists' attention in print.[26] This lacuna may seem strange at first, since comparative literature would appear the one area of literary and cultural studies in which some discussion of pluralism would be inevitable. But my belief is that comparative literature as a discipline has for the most part been left out of pluralism's discourse precisely because it is the one area in which the exclusions practiced by pluralism's problematic of general persuasion become most apparent.

Edward W. Said, a critic whose early work fits in the pluralist mold but who has more recently moved away from pluralist positions, remarked during a round-table discussion at the close of the American Comparative Literature Association's meetings in

March 1986 that there appear to be, among American compara-
tists, two general conceptions of what comparative literature is.[27]
One is that comparative literature is or should be the study of various national literatures, first on their own terms and in their own
sociocultural and sociopolitical contexts — that is, within their
own histories — and then in the broader context of world currents.
This position does not in any sense deny the importance of the
abstraction of theory — indeed, the theoretical apparatus needed to
make sense of such a vast historical/literary project would be the
most sophisticated and the most expansive possible — nor does it
ignore the internationalization of art in various periods, from the
religious and secular texts of the early Middle Ages to the poetry
and music of the seventeenth century to the narrative of our own
era of postmodernism. It does, however, see literary studies as the
inevitably contrastive study of literature in terms of the objective
truths of power and conflict as well as in terms of the subjective
truths of psychological effect and literary craft.

The other view of comparative literature abroad in the land is
the view of the pluralist (though I hasten to add that Said did not
use this term). This view of what comparative literature is or
should be is also the one held by many English departments in
America as well as by many comparative literature programs that
are run, for want of a better term, by or out of English departments. Although this perspective often adopts the mantle of "theory" as opposed to "history" or to (naively objectivist) "historiciz-
ing," its notions both of "history" *and* of "theory" are extremely
limited, in fact limited in just the way that pluralism itself is limited. This view of comparative literature, that literary study is the
study of ahistorical, materially unmotivated texts, the cultural
equivalents of the panoply of notes in the grand ahistorical sym-
phony of world literature, is the realm of potential agreement and
accord. It achieves such agreement, however — as does all pluralist
discourse within the problematic of general persuasion — by means
of *a priori* exclusion of those who would, in the beginning or in the
end, exclude. This pluralist view of comparative literature thus
altogether excludes or brackets the Other (at times in the form of
the departmental Marxist, the departmental feminist, the depart-

mental embodiment of cultural studies, and so on) or, still more often and more insidiously, considers the Other only as a version of the Self. In pedagogical terms, the result of this view is the study of texts at random, stripped of their cultural heritage, and more often than not even stripped of their language, since the standard mode of study (with a few notable exceptions, such as texts in French and, currently, in Spanish) is to read texts only in English translation. Again, the liberal ideology of pluralism is an undeniably powerful force in American literary studies and in American social and political life, and it has not left our universities or our departments and programs of comparative literature untouched.

To return to the Continental opposition with which we began, it should be apparent by now that Derrida, despite American attempts to "domesticate" his thought within the realm of pluralism, is not a pluralist at all. For the time being, suffice it to quote Derrida's response, in 1980, to an interviewer's assertion that deconstruction inevitably leads to pluralist interpretation, thus entailing the problem of the selection of certain interpretations as being somehow better than or superior to others. As Rooney has noticed, Derrida is explicit in rejecting both the label of the pluralist and the pluralist interpretive procedure:

I am not a pluralist, and I would never say that every interpretation is equal but I do not select. The interpretations select themselves. I am a Nietzschean in that sense. You know that Nietzsche insisted on the fact that the principle of differentiation was in itself selective. The eternal return of the same was not repetition, it was a selection of the more powerful forces. So I would not say that some interpretations are truer than others. I would say that some are more powerful than others. The hierarchy is between forces and not between true and false.[28]

Gianni Vattimo, on the other hand, is a pluralist, though his version of pluralism fits within the framework of German philosophy rather than that of American literary and cultural theory. Vattimo's work is thus distinct both from the implicitly exclusionary pluralist tradition of American criticism and from the overtly exclusionary nonpluralist tradition of Italian criticism. Indeed, one of the reasons for the attention that *il pensiero debole* has received in Italy is, it seems to me, the strangeness of Vattimo's fascination for weakly formulated pluralities and pluralist discourse in the midst of a tradition that is not pluralistic. Although Vattimo's importation of some of the strategies and concerns of Derridean deconstruction within a pluralist problematic does make him the "next step" in post-poststructuralist thought in Italy, that does not mean that *il pensiero debole* is without problems. An obvious one, which Vattimo shares with pluralist discourse in general, is the inability, within his programmatically nonauthoritarian thought, to formulate a clear concept of interpretive authority (the recurrent hobgoblin of pluralist discourse), which means that the authoritative exclusions practiced by his thought are usually effected *a priori*. This blindness leads to a second problem, one of both authority and periodization, in the form of Vattimo's lack of a definite and convincing understanding of the difference between the critical self-consciousness of modernism and that of postmodernism. This lack becomes crucial at the end of his *La fine della modernità* (*The End of Modernity*).[29] The ahistorical and idealist slant of Vattimo's discourse leads him to see postmodern self-consciousness as a sort of safety valve rather than an open-ended pathway, a way of preserving the integrity of modernist wholeness (however that wholeness was itself ironized) rather than a way of breaking it apart. Though this is too thorny an issue to be treated in detail here, I do go into it at greater length in another context.[30]

To conclude, I should say that, in contrast to many of my colleagues currently involved in the examination of critical pluralism in the American tradition, I do not regard pluralism as a disguised brand of monism. Its genuinely multiple forms and its manifold if unspoken interests and exclusions make it too complex for that sort of description, which is one of the reasons why it is so hard to put your finger on it. But it is, nonetheless, an ideology, a way inconsistent or not, conscious or not, coherent or not, of viewing human life and human history, and that is, after all, what I have been discussing in these pages.

3

History with a Future(?)

Marxist Criticism in the United States

IN THE UNITED STATES, Marxist literary criticism has had two flowering moments, one in the 1930's, with the polemics and counterpolemics that developed around the coterie now known as the "New York intellectuals," the other in the 1970's and 1980's, with the highly influential and much-debated writings of the group of recent Marxist academic critics and theorists, foremost among them Fredric Jameson.[1] It is true that the gap between these two moments and the criticism they produced is often regarded as impossible to negotiate, a difference conceived of as an unbridgeable chasm rather than as a mere shift in nuance or emphasis. It is also true that this difference is usually attributed — and rightly so, at least in part — to the intervening influence of such momentous international events as the global political crisis and the coming of World War II and of such pervasive local phenomena as the postwar dawning and subsequent rise of McCarthyism. While it would be pointless to deny that there are genuine differences between these two sets of writings, or that the above-mentioned reasons for these differences do in fact apply, it is equally important to see that there are other forces at work here. One is the extraordinary change in the underlying sociopolitical context between the 1930's and the 1980's, specifically the internationalization of culture in the postmodern era and the continuing viability — despite all radical and liberal prognostications of the late 1960's — of conservative pluralism on the postwar American political scene. Another force is the remarkable change in the concept of revolution that has occurred between these two periods in the United States in particular and in the West (including Western Marxism) in general. In coming to grips with these changes, it is helpful to consider what American Marxist criticism has been in the past in order to gauge what it is at present and also what it may be in the future — if, indeed, the conditions for its continued existence can be said to obtain any longer at all.

The Marxist tradition in American writings runs along several tracks, among the more important of these being economics, political science, and sociology. Although Marxist *literary* criticism constitutes both a more recent and a narrower line of inquiry than these others, when that field is expanded to include literary and cultural commentary, the arena in which Marxist critical discourse can be seen to have operated becomes considerably vaster. The primary roots of this sort of commentary, and in fact of all American Marxist thinking, extend back to the turn of the century, specifically to the battles of the nascent labor movement and of political action groups struggling throughout the United States for identity and legitimation. Whether or not the reasoning and the strategies of such early political and labor leaders as W. E. B. Du Bois, Eugene Debs, and William "Big Bill" Haywood were successful in either the short term or the long term, the ways in which these figures approached the problems they faced — within the unions, the party system, and the courts as well as in the violence of the strike and the street — introduced the concepts of Marxist thought to the American public. At the same time, it should be remembered that this was only an introduction and that the Marxist influence in this period was often coupled with problems that, in traditional terms, were not solely Marxist, such as the question of blacks' rights, the recognition of labor unions and union activity within the American political and legal system, and the often strained opposition between skilled craftsmen evincing the classic artisanal mentality of the guild and the increasingly vocal numbers of un- skilled industrial workers.

In the early decades of this century, American Marxist thought focused on a series of sociopolitical and ethical questions within an international framework. The first of these had to do with the controversy over United States's policy regarding World War I, in which the American Marxists were staunchly anti-interventionist. The second, lasting throughout the 1920's and into the 1930's, concerned the attention to and admiration for the institutional growth of the Soviet Union under the leadership of Lenin and then, from the late 1920's into the 1930's, under the hand of Stalin. One of the specifically literary offshoots of this interest was the estab- lishment of the many John Reed clubs, writers' groups formed to work in the memory of the American political and sociocultural critic most closely associated with the October Revolution and its aftermath up until his death in 1920. The third set of questions that drew the reaction of Marxist thinkers in the United States arose in the 1930's, and each of them centered in one way or another on Stalin and his policies: the rigid bureaucratization of the apparatus of the Soviet state under Stalin's rule; the rumors and then the affirmation of the purge trials as vehicles for an internal policy of state terror; and, finally, the dispute between Stalin and Trotsky over national as opposed to international communism, with its implications, so crucial to Western writers, for Western Marxism and for what Trotsky termed "permanent revolution" and with its results in Trotsky's exile from the Soviet Union and the founding of the Fourth International. Through all of these latter issues there runs a unifying thread, a set of basic questions that, succinctly stated, have to do with the concept of revolution: under what sort of conditions can revolution be said to be feasible, how does it actually come into being, and to what sort of economic and socio- political entity might it lead?

In regard to cultural studies proper, it was in this turbulent intel- lectual atmosphere of the 1930's that American Marxism came into its own. It is all too easy today to forget the vitality of the

cultural polemics that were centered in New York in the 1930's —
against the backdrop of the Depression and the New Deal — or to
dismiss the arguments themselves either for their lack of theoretical
sophistication or for their lack of relevance to more contemporary
debates over Marxist concepts. This sort of dismissal is implicit in
the silence on this era that is so striking in current American Marxist writings, an attitude asserted most concisely at the beginning of
the preface to Fredric Jameson's *Marxism and Form* of 1971: "The
burning issues of those days [the 1930's] generated polemics which
we may think back on with nostalgia but which no longer corre-
spond to the conditions of the world today. The criticism practiced
then was of a relatively untheoretical, essentially didactic nature,
destined more for use in the night school than in the graduate sem-
inar, if I may put it that way."[2] Still, even in the midst of Jameson's
sweepingly confident assessment, there appears at least a glimmer
of demurral ("if I may put it that way"), a hesitancy suggesting that
perhaps there *was* something more to this body of criticism — and
to the underlying issues at stake — than is immediately clear from
the way it is treated, or, better, not treated, in the new Marxist
critical writings of the past two decades.

What were the central concerns of the Marxist critics of the
1930's? This was the first opportunity, it should be recalled, for
American Marxist critics to concentrate on questions that were
specifically *literary*, in the contrast between the values and forms of
literary realism and those of literary modernism. True, the background for these controversies included the sociopolitical problems, outlined earlier, stirred up by the disturbing news of the
Soviet purge and the fight between Stalin and Trotsky. But the core
of the literary dispute, as it was played out in the pages of the new
Partisan Review after 1937 (in opposition to the pro-Soviet line
that had been taken by the *New Masses*, the *New Republic*, and
The Nation), concerned the power of literature and culture to
change the way people saw their world and their place in that
world and thus, in Trotsky's terms, the potential of literature itself
not just to reflect society but to help alter society in a truly revolutionary sense.[3]

This debate raged throughout the second half of the 1930's, with many of the more prominent American critics of the day involved in one way or another, Granville Hicks, Mike Gold, and Malcolm Cowley usually arguing for the established Soviet position in favor of realism, Philip Rahv, Dwight Macdonald, William Phillips, Frederick Dupee, Mary McCarthy, and later Sidney Hook and the remainder of the editorial group at the new *Partisan Review* supporting Trotsky and modernism. As socialist realism became Soviet doctrine under Stalin in the 1930's and 1940's, the difference between its program and the literature of modernism became considerably clearer, with the result that Lionel Trilling, the American academic champion of modernism (and eventually liberalism) at Columbia became a sort of unofficial New York arbiter of taste, the counterpart to Zhdanov's cultural dominion in the Soviet Union.[4]

The 1930's debate in New York had important roots in the sociocultural activity of the previous decade, particularly in American writers' involvement in the Sacco-Vanzetti defense campaign and in the Jewish radicalism of the *Menorah Journal*'s editorial group and contributors, as Alan Wald has pointed out.[5] It also spawned significant developments in the subsequent decade (following the 1937 hearings of the Dewey Commission in Mexico and Trotsky's assassination in 1940), developments going well beyond the bounds of Trotsky's influence and the modernist/realist dispute, in the hands of such writers as Edmund Wilson, F. O. Matthiessen, and others.[6] Considering the New York 1930's from another angle, it is equally noteworthy that the disagreements in the United States over the values and tactics of literary modernism had parallels in Europe and in the East, in the form of the often discussed Brecht-Lukács debate in the 1930's and the exchanges between Palmiro Togliatti, Mario Alicata, and Elio Vittorini in the pages of *Rinascita* and *Il Politecnico* in the mid and late Italian 1940's (an exchange delayed in part, no doubt, by the repressive powers of the fascist state).

Beyond the questions of roots, ramifications, and parallels, however, the more compelling issue here is the concern — constant throughout the American 1930's — for the concept of revolution. This concern runs throughout the writings of the New York 1930's from the anti-Stalinist left to the literary apologists for the Soviet regime. As well as in the writings of the *Partisan Review* group, it appears in the locus classicus of 1930's Party writing, Granville Hicks's *The Great Tradition*, at the conclusion of which "revolutionary" writers from Dreiser to Dos Passos (together with authors like Norris, Bellamy, Sinclair, and London) and the revolutionary tradition in which they are said to work are presented as the leading lights of the recent past and the present and as the hopes of the insurgent future.[7] Such prominent members of the opposing faction as Rahv and Macdonald looked back later to affirm the same central "revolutionary" interest, albeit from a polemically modernist perspective.[8] But irrespective of these differences in literary and cultural point of view, the regular attention to the notion of revolution and to the genuine possibility for real cultural *and* sociopolitical change brings these writings into an instructive and forceful (if also heterogeneous) whole.

It is true that the New York intellectuals moved far away from their commitment to the concept of revolution as the decades passed. Wald has traced the arc of this movement in some detail, with special emphasis on the career of Hook but including those of Irving Howe, Max Eastman, Macdonald, Cowley, and many others in a progression that led at times to postwar moderation or liberalism and at times, in the Nixon and Reagan years, to reactionary conservatism. In this context, it is well to recall the publishing career of one of the early members of the New York intellectual community of the Left, Max Eastman, who began as editor of the *Masses* and the *Liberator* before giving voice to a growing skepticism in the exchange between the opposing Marxist factions in the 1920's and 1930's and who, in the 1940's, ended up writing anticommunist tracts and working for *Reader's Digest*. At any rate, whatever the path of development in individual instances, the internecine battles waged throughout American Marxism effectively came to a close with the onset of World War II, and needless to say, they were not reopened afterwards in the Cold War era of McCarthyism and repression.

To a certain extent, it is possible to trace similarities between the development of the Old Left of the 1930's and that of the New Left of the 1960's, at least as regards their beginnings in polemic and enthusiasm and their endings in apathy and/or reaction. But despite the tempting analogies furnished by the late 1960's radical pamphleteers who turned out to be the bankers and stockbrokers of the 1970's and 1980's, it should be remembered that there were also major differences between the 1930's and the 1960's in both intellectual climate and social life. The first of these had to do with the material conditions of life in the United States — the prosperity of the 1960's as distinguished from the grinding poverty and social turmoil of the Depression. These conditions affected the socioeconomic atmosphere and audience of the writers and apologists of both decades, and they had a result of special moment for the American student activists of the late 1960's and early 1970's in that the more vocal activists were primarily the children of the materially comfortable bourgeoisie, free to protest against the involvement in Vietnam precisely because they came from the class that was *not* fighting and dying in the disastrous war in Southeast Asia.

Several further characteristics of the 1960's Left are notable in distinguishing the New Left both from the Old Left of the 1930's (which the student activists of the 1960's tended to denigrate en masse in a generational schema that can only be termed Oedipal) and from the Marxist intellectuals of the 1970's and 1980's, on whom the 1960's radicals seem to have had little lasting effect. Perhaps the most telling, if also the most general, of these characteristics was the cult of individualism — which persisted regardless of repeated attempts at fostering versions of collectivity — that ran throughout the New Left as the ironically pervasive inheritance of its bourgeois capitalist upbringing, with the outcome that even the most committed participants tended to act genuinely as a group only when under attack (a viable strategy for defense but not for originating or carrying out a positive sociopolitical program of any sort). The 1960's radicals remained *protesters*, defined by their relation to a set of present social and economic circumstances, and their revolt remained one of youths against their elders, thus shaping their activities in a relational manner that did not carry the dispute outside the bounds of the original disagreement. When the circumstances changed in the 1970's and the topic of the war ceded to that of Watergate, the former elements of the New Left faded away, returned to the capitalist fold (from which they had withdrawn only partially and only provisionally), or self-destructed in fragmentary acts of nonproductive terrorist violence.

The remarkably complete dissolution of the 1960's Left is due in part to two further factors, each of them again springing from the background of education and social experience that formed so many of the Left's protagonists. Since philosophy as a discipline is rarely if ever present in American secondary schools (or taught only through literature itself), the seemingly radical student groups had virtually no preparation in the sort of Marxist or, more broadly speaking, materialist thought that would have provided a theoretical understanding of what it was they claimed to be all about. Again, this lack of intellectual grounding distinguished the 1960's student radicals *grosso modo* from much of the Old Left of the 1930's. True, in the 1960's there were radical texts in circulation — from short works by Marx and Engels, Lenin, and Mao, to longer ones by Malcolm X and Eldridge Cleaver — and there was a great deal of sloganeering; but there was no very profound theoretical or historical understanding of what in the long run the slogans of the day really meant beyond particular political problems. At the same time, there was a glaring lack of practical experience in sociopolitical organization. The intimacy with political structure and proletarian conflict that had contributed so crucially to the formation of leftist radicals in Europe and in previous decades in the United States, from Lenin, Trotsky, and Gramsci to Debs, Haywood, and Reed, was utterly lacking among the radicals of the American New Left, who could no longer turn either to the party system or to the thoroughly bureaucratized and often politically conservative labor unions for sustenance and instruction. The net result of these historical shortcomings, on theoretical *and* practical planes, was that the revolt of the 1960's remained a slip — an important one, but just a slip — in the development of American society in the time of late capitalism. In the end, the 1960's radicals returned to the patriarchate merely to strengthen the ideology of liberal humanism out of which their rebellion had originally sprung, while, in the process, the focus of American Marxist thought moved away from the streets and into the academy.

This specifically academic context is the one in which, it seems to me, Fredric Jameson's work should be approached. Jameson himself suggests this framework in the prefatory comments to *Marxism and Form* quoted earlier, where he explicitly denies the Marxist writings of the 1930's as constituting any sort of intellectual roots: Jameson's Marxist criticism is of the intellectual stripe, a body of work that is intended for an academic audience rather than the sort of public aimed at by the journalists of the 1930's or the demonstrators of the 1960's. Indeed, even though Jameson's prefatory rejection is aimed overtly at the writers of the 1930's, it could be said that the real thrust of Jameson's remarks is to disengage his works as well from the 1960's (a period he rarely mentions until his more recent writing, especially the essay "Periodizing the 60s").[9] But leaving aside for the moment this kind of intentional amnesia — an affliction common to a curiously large segment of the American Left through the entire postwar period, as Wald's work has helped to point out[10] — it does seem the case not only that Jameson's critical writing is distinguished by its use of non-American traditions and approaches but also that a good measure of its value lies in this European-influenced Hegelian and Marxist slant.[11]

Although several figures of some significance are currently writing on contemporary culture from a broadly Marxist perspective — the name of Frank Lentricchia comes quickly to mind, as does that of Stanley Aronowitz — no one over the last twenty years or so has had anywhere near the influence that Jameson has had. Through his books and essays of the 1970's and 1980's, Jameson has introduced an entire generation of younger American critics to the enticements of Marxist criticism and theory. Because of his works' massive influence and because of their complexity, it might be best to treat them in some detail before attempting to position them and their implications in regard to American Marxist criticism overall. Already in *Marxism and Form*, a work that treats principally Marxist cultural theorists rather than literary works themselves, many of the salient traits of Jameson's style and point of view are on open display. Throughout, Jameson insists on what he terms "dialectical" (or, roughly, critically self-conscious) thought while retaining the traditional infrastructure/superstructure model, with both its attendant appeal to reflection theory, albeit handled by Jameson in an extraordinarily flexible way, and its eventual recourse to seemingly hidden but no less powerful Lukácsian totalities. His writing also evinces his characteristic choice of authors and subject matter, usually with a French and German bias (here Theodor Adorno, Walter Benjamin, Herbert Marcuse, Friedrich von Schiller, Ernst Bloch, Georg Lukács, and Jean-Paul Sartre) but occasionally Anglo-American as well. At every stage of his argument, moreover, one sees the dynamism that propels both the form and the content of Jameson's work, with its impulse, on the level of critical procedure, to try out as many different approaches as possible within an ordered critical discourse, and its explicit statement, on the level of critical belief, that what literature reflects is not so much the static or mechanically predictable interests of class, as had been true, for example, for Georgi Plekhanov and even for Lucien Goldmann, but the ideological content of ongoing class *struggle*.[12]

In *The Political Unconscious* (1981), Jameson's cultural interests and theoretical assertions are much the same, but his focus on literature, here first on the roots of the novel in romance and then on both the realism of Balzac and Gissing and the early modernism of Conrad, is considerably more consistent. After the book's polemical introductory section (e.g., the exhortation "Always historicize!"), Jameson embarks on an exposition of his theory of narrative interpretation, in the course of which he sets forth the three "progressively wider horizons" of critical analysis: first, the individual text as a *symbolic act*; second, the sociocultural context of the work in question, in which the semantic units of investigation are no longer single texts but the "ideologemes" of the "essentially antagonistic collective discourses of social classes"; and, third, the broadest horizon of cultural study, what Jameson terms "the ideology of form, that is, the symbolic messages transmitted to us by the coexistence of various sign systems which are themselves traces or anticipations of modes of production."[13] The movement from one area of concern to the next (all of which areas, it should be noted, involve questions of content as well as form) then provides the model both for the progression within the individual chapters and, more generally, for the study as a whole as it proceeds from the origins of European narrative, through the nineteenth-century novel's development in the hands of Alessandro Manzoni, Stendhal, and particularly Honoré de Balzac, and up to the threshold of high modernism.

Throughout *The Political Unconscious*, Jameson's aim is to recover the driving forces of the political and social contradictions of human life as they take shape in narrative, however obscure, indirect, layered, or "sedimented" (a concept he adopts from Husserl) those forces and their effects may be. The unmasking and restoration of these underlying energies — which, as in Jameson's three concentric horizons, always lead in the final analysis to the relation between social classes and the modes of production — are the proper roles of interpretive criticism, the sort of criticism that is necessarily concerned with both history (in Jameson's algebra, "History itself") and theory, and thus, finally, with ideology. These articles of intellectual faith, when accompanied by the explicit proposals for analytic procedure, provide Jameson's discourse with an ordered hierarchy of interests — a hierarchy determined and refined in large part by the thought of Sartre, Lukács, the Frankfurt School, and Louis Althusser (read, interestingly enough, as only in part a structuralist) but also influenced by Gramsci and by recent American socioeconomic and anthropological theorists. This hierarchy tends to keep Jameson's analyses headed along a distinct if multileveled sociopolitical path; and this is so even when the objects proposed for discussion are the state, law, and the question of nations, as at the end of *The Political Unconscious*, or the status of culture in postmodern America and in the third world, as in several of Jameson's essays. In other words, whether Jameson's analytical concern is focused, as in his earlier works, on individual texts and thinkers in the guise of "metacommentary" or, as in his later essays, on the broader cultural phenomena of "transcoding,"[14] with its more overt emphasis on the often *antagonistic* interdisciplinary questions of objectivity and subjectivity and of quantity and quality, Jameson's thought strives to remain true to its Marxist heritage even as it manages to interrogate in pluralist fashion a spectacular array of critical protocols and strategies.

To return for a moment to *The Political Unconscious*, we might conclude discussion of Jameson's work by noting a pair of interconnected difficulties. The first of these has to do with the relation between the literary text and the political unconscious (which Jameson sees in its historical garb as a massive but also "absent" cause), while the second has to do with the relation between Jameson's interpretive system *as* a system and the texts that he discusses in the course of his analyses. Despite all Jameson's attempts to bring order to his work, each of these relations can be regarded in practice, from a generous perspective, as fluid, or, from a more critical perspective, as simply vague. In each case, even though the various elements of the equation are clear in the abstract, the functional relation between them ends up cloudy. There is, of course, a good reason for this. Whereas Jameson favors a new and full allegorical criticism, rich in its sociopolitical and cultural suppositions as well as in its critical repertoire, he obviously opposes the reductive, mechanistic allegories of the kind indulged in by much of the earlier Marxist criticism in Europe and in the United States. Both the fleet-footedness of Jameson's own treatment of the relations between economy, politics, and culture and the stunning pluralism of his analytic procedures point up his desire to avoid reductionism — be it of the economic cast or any other — at the same time that they demonstrate, for now, the weakness inherent in his system-making. In the previous chapter, I mentioned Jameson's pluralism in the sense of the multiple meanings of "the political" itself. This pluralism is oddly connected to his ongoing adhesion to Marxist reflection theory so evident in his book *Postmodernism*, in which many differing perspectives are adopted to demonstrate, at the end, that postmodern culture is still playing the reflective tune of the international bourgeois economy.[15] True, in this book Jameson is at times somewhat more generous and even more flexible than in earlier ones, but the message, as I have pointed out elsewhere, remains fundamentally the same.[16] At this juncture, I would simply add that, irrespective of the ambiguities of Jameson's position, if plural-

ism is Jameson's weakness it is also his strength, for it has made his
writing as compelling and as provocative on a diversity of fronts as
anything that the newer, more theoretical group of critics in the
United States has yet encountered on home ground.

Even this cursory description of the central concerns of Jameson's work should suggest what element of Marxism, in general
and in particular regarding the history of Marxist thought in the
United States, he appears to have left out. That element, is, of
course, the traditional Marxist concern for revolution. Nor does
this lacuna exist solely in Jameson's work: recent writings, influential and engaging, by critics as different from Jameson and from
each other as Richard Ohmann and Michael Ryan show the same
lack of interest in revolution as either a theoretical principle or a
practical goal.[17] True, the term "revolutionary" has had as wide a
variety of meanings in American as in European leftist thought,
from Hicks's 1930's view of socially oriented realist writers to
Rahv's and Macdonald's championing of the antagonistic authors
of modernism and the avant-garde (authors who, in this sense,
suggested the sort of "revolution of the mind" attributed by Jack
Roth to André Breton and the French surrealists), to the "revolutionary" culture of the late 1960's and early 1970's.[18] But differences in definition and conception aside, the concern itself, as a
driving force, is largely absent from contemporary Marxist critical
writing in the United States.

The main question that this situation raises has significant implications for anyone interested in Marxist criticism in the West: is
it sufficient for "Marxist" criticism to remain purely at the level of
analysis rather than to expand so as to include a prescription for
genuine change? In other words, for criticism to be accurately described as Marxist, is it enough that it use the traditional Marxist
analytic categories of economic and sociopolitical thought in order
to describe how such categories can be said to figure in the literary
and cultural texts under examination? If the presuppositions of
this question lead us back to the often virulent critiques launched
against the economistic thinkers of the Second International, they
can also be seen as having functioned closer to home, in the disagreement over the sufficiency of the analysis of such economically

oriented liberal historians of American society as Charles and Mary Beard. Finally, to frame this question in a slightly different way, does a materialist version of American pluralism really constitute a Marxist critical praxis?

To be fair, I should point out that both Jameson and the cultural historian Stanley Aronowitz have acknowledged the dangers of Marxist criticism's falling back into economism.[19] Moreover, each of them offers an anticipatory perspective — however fleetingly — on revolution as an object of thought and of intellectual responsibility. Aronowitz sees revolution as something for which the underdeveloped social and intellectual community in the United States must be diligently prepared through the educational process provided by Marxist analysis; Jameson sees it as an inevitable, if distant, fact on the worldwide social and cultural horizon, a reality that will necessarily be realized as the forces of global capitalism continue to develop and so to create, willy nilly, their own forces of global resistance.[20] But it must also be said that in neither of these writers, nor in their colleagues in academic Marxist criticism, is the attention to questions of revolution especially consistent or thoroughgoing; rather, it usually functions as a kind of professorial footnote or addendum, situated as an introductory or concluding gesture and designed to keep the "revolutionary" aspect of this brand of criticism alive even while the critics themselves are not particularly occupied with it.

It is of interest here to note the predilection that Jameson, Aronowitz, and their contemporary American Marxist critics have shown for the work of Antonio Gramsci (a thinker discussed further in subsequent chapters), who is most often considered by these critics as a founding father of the theory of cultural revolution in the West, a variety of revolution that can start with culture as a superstructural phenomenon that will itself influence or even shape its neighboring superstructural categories as well as the workings of the socioeconomic base (though Jameson is well aware of the potentially dangerous slipperiness of this and related positions).[21] It is heartening to see the current regard for Gramsci's thoughts on hegemony, on the formation of the *blocco storico* or "historical block" of social domination, on the gradual revolutionary war of position as opposed to the violent war of movement modeled on the Soviet design, and on the genuine power of culture in society. But it nonetheless gives one pause to see these concepts marshaled to argue, however subtly or indirectly, that perhaps revolution can be effected without recourse to the direct control of the modes of production — an argument that Gramsci, with his background in the northern Italian factory councils and his adherence to what he termed the philosophy of praxis, never considered.

The next question, it would seem, is whether or not such a possibility *should* be considered, which is another way of asking whether or not revolution is currently possible in the United States, and, if so, to what extent Marxist literary and cultural commentators may or may not be able to play a part in it through their work. This is exactly the question, of course, for which at present there is no answer and for which there probably cannot be from any academic perspective, whether oriented by economics, history, the social sciences, or literary criticism. Some approaches to this topic seem to me even less appropriate and less fruitful than others. One of the least helpful of them is embodied in an anthology meant to document the presence of Marxist influence in American academics, *The Left Academy,* a work undoubtedly conceived sometime in the late 1970's but published in 1982, at the height, ironically, of the success of what has on occasion been called the "Reagan revolution."[22] With such self-confident and self-congratulatory friends and apologists as the contributors to *The Left Academy*, Marxist thinkers looking toward real change, as opposed to academic window-dressing easily assimilable into the institutional mainstream, have little need of enemies. A more instructive approach seems to me to be the one sketched out by Edward Said — interestingly enough, a critic who *is* of the historicist persuasion but who is avowedly not a Marxist — in the course of his collection *The World, the Text, and the Critic* and in particular in his comments on what he terms "American 'Left' Literary Criticism."[23] Said's doubts about the genuinely adversarial nature of American "Left" criticism (whence the quotation marks in his title) extend to the lamentable lack of revisionist studies in American literary history and to the not only traditional but also continuing isolation of literary studies from the world of social life. Although, as will become clearer in the next chapter, I do not endorse every facet of Said's position — his arguments concerning both Harold Bloom and Paul de Man, for example, strike me now as having dated very quickly — his statements regarding the need for leftist criticism to consider seemingly extraneous but nevertheless related, or in Said's terminology, "affiliated," facts of social life and his skeptical, implicitly challenging stance toward his topic appear to hit the mark today just as much as before.

Why and how is such continuing skepticism warranted? By comparison to the question about the current viability of revolution in the United States, this one is considerably less difficult to address, although, in the end, both questions lead back into the same path of investigation. In sociopolitical terms, the first place to look for an answer, needless to say, is the outcome of the presidential elections of the past twenty-five years — well into the era in which the generation of voters supposedly radicalized by the teachings of "the Left academy" had attained the age of voting rights — elections not once resulting in a Left or even liberal (as opposed to middle-of-the-road) majority. Indeed there are some grounds to believe that the presence of the Left in the faculty rolls of the American university may function much as the presence of the leftist academic community and even of the (now fragmented) Communist Party has often functioned in the course of sociopolitical life in postwar Italy, which is to say as a safety valve incorporated into the system not to overturn or destroy it but rather to permit it to continue working as before without major disruption. In other words, what is at times viewed as the prospective utopian allegory of radical thought in American institutions of higher learning (in the views of Alan Bloom, E. D. Hirsch, and others) may turn out to be the irony of that thought's effective paralysis in any sort of sociopolitical action.

Several further reasons for skepticism regarding the concept of revolution on the current American Left have to do with the differences alluded to at the outset of this chapter between the 1930's and the 1980's. Although the roots of these differences can be traced in part to World War II, neither the war nor the period of

McCarthyism that followed are sufficient to explain them. First among these differences, mentioned earlier in the context of the 1960's, is the relatively advanced state of material life in the United States at present. It is true that even into the 1990's there do exist glaring exceptions to the standards of comfort and well-being enjoyed by most Americans—the migrant labor population in rural areas, the unemployed of American urban centers and in particular of their ghettos—but the overall level of material comfort is such that revolution arising from lack of the basic necessities of life seems an increasingly unlikely prospect.

The second of these differences, mentioned by critics and theorists from Said to Samuel Weber to Jameson, is the retreat of American leftist discourse onto the reservation of the academy, with all the institutional restrictions that such a reservation imposes, whether overtly or covertly, from the tenure system to departmental organization to classroom duties and course review.[24] The third difference, also suggested previously, is to be found in the internationalization of the market system—with effects on the production and sale not only of commodities but also of culture—with its global network of interconnecting financial operations and communications making any genuine desire for revolutionary practice only an unrealizable goal when tied to purely local or even national revolutionary drives, at least outside the countries of what used to be termed the third world. In the United States, then—a nation with a predominantly satisfied proletariat, with no tradition of a broadly based revolutionary political party, and so with no real institutional ground for the Left except perhaps the university; a nation in which social analysis of Lukácsian "reification" quickly slips to notions of "alienation" and thence to Durkheimian "anomie," in which economic perspectives are increasingly focused on global phenomena, and in which academic discussion of the failure of Marxist concepts and prospects offers only one more excuse "to wait and see"— revolution, for the present, appears as remote on the social horizon as it ever has in any of the decades following the 1930's.

Given these circumstances, along with the worldwide collapse of so-called Marxist regimes, it might seem that the time has come for the Left in the United States to abandon the idea of revolution and to jettison the pretense of Marxist criticism along with it. However, while I do think that fundamental reconsideration is in order, I do not believe that such total abnegation is either necessary or advantageous, and neither, it would seem, does Jameson. Jameson's usual tack in dealing with this sort of question is to divide Marxist criticism along two lines, the one concerned with ideological analysis, the other with utopian possibilities, and then to concentrate on the former, as we have seen, even while giving some (albeit brief) acknowledgment to the latter. In this regard, it is worth remembering the precisely phrased and stirring conclusions of both *Marxism and Form* and *The Political Unconscious*. But this open call to arms, in the appeal not only to history but indeed to analysis of historical ideology so as to be able to think of history's utopian *future* — albeit without consideration of transitional revolutionary steps — is not the only strategy adopted in Jameson's more recent writings. In an essay of 1985, "Architecture and the Critique of Ideology,"[25] Jameson works out a scheme, however tentative, with an eye toward a Marxist cultural praxis that would be neither a laissez-faire, postmodern version of self-satisfied "cultural" revolution nor a single-minded return to Marxist revolutionary categories of the past — including even the not so distant past leading up to 1968. It is especially significant, first, that Jameson constructs his position in this essay with explicit reference to Gramsci's thought — seen in a specifically materialist perspective, at once practical *and* principled, in direct opposition to the way Gramscian analysis and appeal has often been "used" by both the Italian and the American Left — and, second, that he does so in the vein not so much of criticism as of comparative cultural *commentary* (to use a word that has been debased in recent decades in the United States but that as I said before should be reinstituted in its broadly antagonistic sense), that is, comparative analysis of the present with a practical eye to the future. For the moment, naturally, it remains to be seen just how deeply these new positions will be held, either by Jameson or by his colleagues.

In conclusion, I offer no brief here for a nostalgic repetition of the American Marxist criticism of the 1930's, but I do suggest a review of the issues of cultural power and revolution in which those writers were so thoroughly steeped. Otherwise, the lessons of that decade and of the 1960's will be lost to us, lessons that should indicate to what a notable extent intellectuals of the Left in the United States continue to participate, like it or not, in the very sociocultural systems that they are intent on analyzing and changing. This is to say that any genuine revolution will of necessity be "against" not just our interlocutors and opponents but also, in an institutional sense, "against" ourselves, our institutionalized ways of thinking and acting, our currently established frames of sociopolitical and cultural reference. Here, of course, I am deliberately recasting Said's dual trajectory of filiation in critical history and affiliation in sociocultural commentary, with a view to understanding the heritage of Marxist thought in the United States in order to avoid repeating its failures. This is also a way of coming to terms with the contemporary pervasiveness of the forces of culture, particularly the unifying nature of capitalist-produced mass culture, in order, through cultural critique, to unmask the illusions of unity at the heart of the fetishistic workings of mass culture itself. If in the end it turns out that none of this proves sufficient, that cultural commentary, however perceptive or engaged, is unequal to the task of carrying out the program of education *and* action at hand, it may be that another return to Gramscian thought really will be needed before Marxist criticism as commentary can become — be it in a traditional or in an authentically innovative guise — *praxis*.

4

"Could you elaborate on that?"
(Well, Yes and No)

The Use and Abuse of Gramsci in Said, Spivak, and Recent Cultural Studies

In CULTURAL STUDIES, the question persists as to what the differences are, if there are differences, between descriptive and programmatic (not to say hortatory) analysis. Often these two sorts of discourse—the descriptive discourse of "this is" as opposed to the programmatic discourse of "this is and this should be"—are mixed together within cultural studies. This situation is not especially strange given that cultural studies itself is a new and growing and, to put it mildly, ebullient field, the kind of field that admits and even invites the dynamic of disarray that contributes to intellectual growth. Nonetheless it seems clear by now that this very growth, if it is to be both meaningful and salutary, ought to occur in an atmosphere not only of intellectual enthusiasm but also of intellectual rigor. One minor though extremely instructive example of this central atmospheric problem within cultural studies can be found in the use of the work of Antonio Gramsci by Edward Said, Gayatri Spivak, and others, and specifically the use of a passage by Gramsci that, thanks to Said, has become a locus classicus as regards the nexus of thought and action, which is to say of theory and practice, in literary and cultural investigation today.[1]

I have discussed Said's work earlier in other contexts, but here I want to concentrate specifically on Said's use of Gramsci. The Gramscian passage in question is found in the eleventh notebook of the critical edition of Gramsci's *Quaderni del carcere* (*Prison Notebooks*) and in English translation in *Selections from the Prison Notebooks*.[2] As quoted by Said in his "Reflections on American 'Left' Literary Criticism," the passage reads as follows (the ellipsis is Said's):

What must . . . be explained is how it happens that in all periods there co-exist many systems and currents of philosophic thought, how these currents are born, how they are diffused, and why in the process of diffusion they fracture along certain lines and in certain directions. The fact of this process goes to show how necessary it is to order in a systematic, coherent and critical fashion one's own intuitions of life and the world, and to determine exactly what is to be understood by the word "systematic," so that it is not taken in the pedantic and academic sense. But this elaboration must be, and can only be, performed in the context of the history of philosophy, for it is this history which shows how thought has been elaborated over the centuries and what a collective effort has gone into the present method of thought which has subsumed and absorbed all this past history, including all its follies and mistakes. Nor should those mistakes themselves be neglected, for, although made in the past and since corrected, one cannot be sure that they will not be reproduced in the present and once again require correcting.[3]

The full text from Gramsci in the Italian original reads as follows:

Occorre dunque spiegare come avviene che in ogni tempo coesistono molti sistemi e correnti di filosofia, come nascono, come si diffondono, perché nella diffusione seguono certe linee di frattura e certe direzioni ecc. Ciò mostra quanto sia necessario sistemare criticamente e coerentemente le proprie intuizioni del mondo e della vita, fissando con esattezza cosa deve intendersi per "sistema" perché non sia capito nel senso pedantesco e professorale della parola. Ma questa elaborazione deve essere e può solo essere fatta nel quadro della storia della filosofia che mostra quale elaborazione il pensiero abbia subìto nel corso dei secoli e quale sforzo collettivo sia costato il nostro attuale modo di pensare che riassume e compendia tutta questa storia passata, anche nei suoi errori e nei suoi delirii, che, d'altronde, per essere stati commessi nel passato ed essere stati corretti non è detto non si riproducano nel presente e non domandino di essere ancora corretti.

Said fixes upon the use in this passage of what he views as a crucial term, *elaborare,* or "to elaborate." Said explains this term as functioning in two ways, first as the elaboration or explication of an existent view of things and second as an indication that culture is a complex and dense entity connected of necessity to political reality. Because Said's own thought here is relatively complex—and in this he echoes the complexity of the Gramscian text from which he cites—it might be appropriate, in all fairness, to quote Said's own summary of his reactions:

First, to elaborate means to refine, to work out (*e-laborare*) some prior or more powerful idea, to perpetuate a world view. Second, to elaborate means something more qualitatively positive, the proposition that culture itself or thought or art is a highly complex and quasi-autonomous extension of political reality and, given the extraordinary importance attached by Gramsci to intellectuals, culture, and philosophy, it has a density, complexity, and historical-semantic value that is so strong as to make politics possible. Elaboration is the ensemble of patterns making it feasible for a society to maintain itself. Far from denigrating elaboration to the status of ornament, Gramsci makes it the very reason for the strength of what he calls civil society, which in the industrial West plays a role no less important than that of political society. Thus elaboration is the central cultural activity and, whether or not one views it as little more than intellectual propaganda for ruling-class interests, it is the material making a society a society. In other words, elaboration is a great part of the social web of which George Eliot spoke in her late novels. Gramsci's insight is to have recognized that subordination, fracturing, diffusing, reproducing, as much as producing, creating, forcing, guiding, are all necessary aspects of elaboration.[4]

In point of fact Gramsci actually signifies something somewhat different by his unthematized and unhighlighted use of the standard Italian term *elaborazione,* which means, first and last, "elaboration," the nominal form of the verb "to elaborate." While it is true that *elaborare* does have the metaphorical equivalent that Said gives to it, "to work out," it is *not* true—outside of the sort of linguistic transformations that regularly occur when words from one language are moved to another, transplantations enlivening metaphorical roots that in the original are, or have become, completely normalized—that the term "elaborate" has any degree of the weight Said gives to it. Two more points should quickly be made, both having to do with discursive contexts. First, Said puts a great deal of emphasis on this single word in the context of what I regard as several of his most principled and most enlightening paragraphs on Gramscian thought and much more importantly on the sorts of failings that Said attributes to American "Left" literary criticism, that is, the seemingly avant-garde (but often sociopolitically retrograde) criticism of the 1970's. This is another way of saying that Said might get the Gramscian term wrong or partly wrong, but he gets the overall sense of Gramsci's thought basically right. Said is serious about Gramsci, has read him long and well, and has done yeoman's service in introducing Gramsci to an American public (although I will have more to say about the outlines of that introduction in the comments to come). The second point is that the context of Gramsci's own text should be borne in mind here.

But before we get to that general context I should say in greater detail just what it is in this section of Gramsci's notebooks that Gramsci intends by the multivalenced term *elaborazione* (that is, for what it is worth, the *noun* that Gramsci actually uses here, *not* the verb *elaborare*). In this passage, Gramsci means two things. To start with the second, he means the elaborate path or network of paths that various forms of thought have taken in the course of the history of thought or philosophy and that therefore shape the way we think about things today. The other meaning that Gramsci sets forth is the elaboration that we make in examining or focusing our own intuitions of the world and of life, thus creating not just a current or path but also a "system" of philosophical understanding of our present situation, which is to say the situation that is constructed for us by the labyrinth of previous history and thought in which we, too, now find ourselves. To repeat, these two meanings of "elaboration" in this passage are not exceptional in either semantic terms as regards Gramsci's Italian or in substantive terms as regards his thinking overall.

Why, then, should Said choose this passage as his central example of Gramsci in this important essay? One of the reasons for this choice, it seems to me, has to do with the amenability of the passage itself to Said's restatement both of Gramsci's positions and of Said's own notions of the relationship between criticism and politics, notions continued in Said's more recent work on Yeats and "decolonialization." A second possible reason for Said's interest in this Gramscian passage — though here I am engaging in pure speculation — may well have to do with the astounding affinity that this section of Gramsci's notebooks demonstrates to the thought of another Italian thinker equally crucial both for Gramsci and for Said, Giambattista Vico.[5] Nonetheless, to return to the question of context, it might be more interesting to consider not just this passage from Gramsci's notebooks but also the passages that precede and follow it (yet to which Said makes no reference whatsoever).

These paragraphs are reproduced in full and accurate translation in Quinton Hoare and Geoffrey Smith's edition. It is true that Said takes his reading of this chosen paragraph to lengths that are, in strict relation to Gramsci's thought as expressed in *these* sentences, nothing short of absurd, which is to say that although Gramsci's thought in general does sustain Said's notion of the importance and the effect of culture, Gramsci's use of the term *elaborare* here and elsewhere in his writings simply does not wield the force that Said gives to it. But again let us look at the context in which this paragraph is found and at the more pressing question of what these paragraphs *in toto* are all about. This context is suggested, however obliquely, in Said's quotation itself, or more precisely in the ellipsis following the second word of Said's citation. What Said leaves out in Gramsci's text and puts into his own in the form of three dots is, in Italian, the word *dunque*, "therefore," a word translated freely though not incorrectly by Hoare and Smith as "next." The result of course is that in Said's text Gramsci's paragraph seems to stand more or less on its own, whereas in the *Quaderni* and in the English translation it only functions as the middle term in a series of propositions that combine to form one overall argument which is not aimed primarily at the history of philosophy as such or at academics in the usual acceptation of that term but rather at the unity of philosophy and politics. For Gramsci, this unity stands, on balance, not as a theoretical question but rather as a practical one. The paragraph immediately preceding the one cited by Said has to do with the ties between philosophy, politics, and action and the relationships that these have with *malafede,* or "bad faith," with respect to individuals and with respect to the communal *vita di larghe masse,* the "life of the great masses," where the concept of *malafede* is, for Gramsci, inadequate, in the sense of the profoundest contrasts between the praxis of social life and ideological commitment. The paragraph directly following the one Said chooses to cite picks up the practical distinctions between philosophy, "good sense," and vulgar philosophy, which are shortly thereafter, in subsequent paragraphs, developed by way of a typical Gramscian formula as the distinctions between *filosofia, buon senso,* and *senso comune* (paragraphs 14 and 15). The point of this later discussion is to define what Gramsci really means not just by philosophy but also by what he terms the philosophy of praxis.

What is it then that we can find hiding under Said's ellipsis? Located here is nothing short of the outline of the system of philosophy that Gramsci wanted to construct in order to lead away from the view of philosophy as a system or systems of thought taken "in the pedantic and academic sense" ("nel senso pedantesco e professorale della parola"). Why is it, we should ask, that in the midst of an argument built to demolish the notion of philosophy as a merely academic or intellectual function, Said chooses to cite — in an intentionally *non*contextual fashion — only the paragraph that is in itself, though *not* if one considers the entire context, the most idealistically philosophical and academic of all the paragraphs of this section in Gramsci's work? However enticing this question may be, rather than rushing to an answer, it might be best at this point to turn to the way a follower of Said adopts this same passage in another discussion of literary theory and cultural studies in the contemporary academy. That critic is Gayatri Spivak, and the works I want to take up are her "Subaltern Studies: Deconstructing Historiography" and "Can the Subaltern Speak?"[6]

The more substantial and meaningful of Spivak's references to Gramsci occur in the first of these two essays, initially published in 1985. Toward the beginning of that essay, Spivak returns to Said's elaboration of Gramsci's text in *The World, the Text, and the Critic* and specifically to Said's recourse to Gramsci's use of the term *elaborare*. Spivak does so in the context of her critique of the Subaltern Studies collective, a group for which she admits a certain admiration even while she faults them for perceiving "their task as making a theory of consciousness or culture rather than specifically a theory of change."[7] This shortcoming is significant for Spivak because she feels that, if the group had passed beyond their traditional conceptual limitations and their excessively sober tone to understand how close they really were to a deconstructive "theory of change," they would have provided a genuine contribution to subaltern studies in a deconstructive mode and conceived of their own critical practice, in all its potential force, in a more convincing manner. What Spivak then says, by means of reference to Gramsci (which quickly thereafter leads to further reference to Nietzsche), is this:

A theory of change as the site of the displacement of function between sign-systems — which is what they [the Subaltern Studies collective] oblige me to read in them — is a theory of reading in the strongest possible general sense. The site of displacement of the function of signs is the name of reading as active transaction between past and future. This transactional reading as (the possibility of) action, even at its most dynamic, is perhaps what Antonio Gramsci meant by "elaboration," *e-laborare*, working out.[5] If seen in this way, the work of the Subaltern Studies group repeatedly makes it possible for us to grasp that the concept-metaphor of the "social text" is not the reduction of real life to the page of a book. My theoretical intervention is a modest attempt to remind us of this.[8]

This reference to Gramsci is not the only one in Spivak's essay; a short while later, Spivak knits together Marx's notion of self-determination in "unalienated practice" and Gramsci's concept of necessary negation in the achievement of self-awareness among the lower classes. But again, the really substantial reference to Gramsci, the one genuine attempt to adopt Gramsci's thought directly within her own discourse, is Spivak's reference to the notion of *elaborare* cited here.

I have already said that Gramsci's use of the verb *elaborare* is not nearly as momentous or as impregnated with significance as Said believes. But the problem in Spivak's essay does not have so much to do with the term's significance — that is, with the term as a concept — as with the very reference itself. To put the point succinctly: what (the devil) is this reference to Gramsci doing here at all?

One thing it is certainly *not* doing in any useful fashion is referring to Gramsci's thought as expressed and developed, or elaborated, in his writings. Undoubtedly, Spivak has heard Gramsci's name in connection with "praxis philosophy," a well-known strand of philosophical, political, and social thought in England and elsewhere in recent decades, and this link would, at least in the logic of academic name dropping, permit her to insert a reference to Gramsci via Said, however superficial such a reference might be, in a paragraph that deals with the "actual *practice*" (albeit in a cultural and critical sense) of the Subaltern Studies group and with the theoretical possibility of reading as "*action . . .* at its most dynamic" (my italics). But even that excuse seems thin at best, since none of this bears more than a passing resemblance to Said's programmatic analysis of "elaboration," much less to Gramsci's use of the term. Certainly, taking a hint from Said's gloss of verbal meaning ("to work out [*e-laborare*]") in order to extend that gloss to a more easily disseminated nominal form (" 'elaboration,' *e-laborare*, working out"), does provide an intriguing twist to Spivak's work by way of the efficacy of sloganeering. The pseudo-Marxian concept of "working out" can thus be seen as a step forward from the authentically Freudian concept of "working through." In other words, the earlier Freudian/Lacanian call to the analytic — and endless — "working through" of the formation and the meaning of the symbol (a phrase that quickly became the darling of psychologically oriented analysis on the part of Spivak and her primarily francophone confreres in the middle years of deconstruction's introduction into the American academy) may thus give way to the teleologically slanted and seemingly practical "working *out*" of 1980's American Marxist criticism. This phrase not only heightens the *telos* of analysis but also stresses the labor of that very process, thus legitimizing the sort of academic enterprise that the editors of *Marxism and the Interpretation of Culture* (in which Spivak's other essay cited above first appeared) can describe without a flinch as "very much a culmination and *working out* of discussions and disputes."[9] By this time, Spivak and others have launched the term, and it has taken. But I do not want to lose the central focus on Spivak's own work, which offers more than enough of an analytic quandary to dwell on. Indeed, in Spivak's essay, the occurrence of "Gramsci" and "elaborare" here reminds one of the parlor game in which a supposedly identical phrase is whispered into the ear of each subsequent player in the circle, so that what starts out as a "bush" in Gramsci becomes a "Christmas tree" in Said and then "Old St. Nick" in Spivak. But a bush and Santa Claus, by these or any other names via displacement or metonomy, are not the same thing, and sooner or later we must confront that fact.

In the process of such a confrontation, we should try to see if there might not be another reason for Spivak's otherwise inexplicable reference. In this search for meaning, Spivak's use of footnotes is at least as helpful as Said's use of ellipsis was previously. In the section of Spivak's essay cited earlier, the notion of a theory of change leads to that of a theory of reading "in the strongest possible general sense . . . as active transaction between past and future," which then leads, via the term "transactional reading," to Gramsci and footnote number five, in which, rather than to Gramsci, the citation refers to Said's treatment of *elaborare* discussed above. Spivak's next reference to Gramsci a short while later is also graced with a footnote, though this time the reference is again not immediately to Gramsci but rather to Gramsci by way of Ranajit Guha's treatment of Gramsci in Guha's *Elementary Aspects of Peasant Insurgency in Colonial India* (1983). The indirection of these references is noteworthy, but indirection in and of itself is hardly the whole story here, since in Spivak's other essay under consideration, "Can the Subaltern Speak?," Gramsci is indeed cited directly, even if the Gramscian work at hand, "Some Aspects of the Southern Question," comes from Gramsci's earlier writings, the essays preceding his imprisonment and his extensive work on the prison notebooks.[10] Spivak's citation of Gramsci occurs in the following terms in the putatively "Gramscian" section of "Can the Subaltern Speak?":[11]

Antonio Gramsci's work on the "subaltern classes" extends the class-position/class-consciousness argument isolated in *The Eighteenth Brumaire*. Perhaps because Gramsci criticizes the vanguardistic position of the Leninist intellectual, he is concerned with the intellectual's role in the subaltern's cultural and political movement into the hegemony. This movement must be made to determine the production of history as narrative (of truth). In texts such as "The Southern Question," Gramsci considers the movement of historical-political economy in Italy within what can be seen as an allegory of reading taken from or prefiguring an international division of labor.[38]

There is considerably less to take exception to in this instance of Spivak's references to Gramsci than in the previously cited example. True, in this general context of the "subaltern" a great deal could have been made of the extraordinarily significant shifts in Gramsci's opinions about the "subalternity" of the Italian south (his homeland) in relation to the Italian north and of Italy as a whole in relation to the rest of Europe and to the international community, as these relations bear on Italy's preparation — or lack of it — for revolution. But this sort of historical framework is not really what concerns Spivak here, and her comments on Gramsci's thought, while remarkably unnuanced, are *grosso modo* unexceptionable. Again, however, what draws attention is less Spivak's commentary on Gramsci's work as such than her footnote, here number 38. As stated above, this note refers to Gramsci's writings of the mid-1920's, but it also includes, almost as an afterthought, another reference, one intended to clear up Spivak's *local* use of the term "allegory" in the phrase "allegory of reading." But it clears up a great deal more than this, for it casts across to her reference to Gramsci in "Deconstructing Historiography" as well as to her entire usage of what can only be termed (as Tony Bennett's recent work guardedly reminds us) a sort of subaltern hero turned cultural superstar, that is, Antonio Gramsci himself in his Anglo-Saxon moment of rediscovery, or, perhaps better, resurrection.

The second reference in note 38 is neither to Said nor to Guha but rather to that marvelous cogitator of both allegories and reading, Paul de Man. Although this combination — Gramsci and de Man — may seem odd even in the light of Spivak's notoriously eclectic (and, to my mind, often astoundingly successful) groupings of intellectual touchstones, the real point here is the perfectly understandable logic of what is not so much a pairing as a form of dual references running along separate tracks. Despite the fact that such a division is neither simple nor clear-cut, the first of these tracks can be described as having to do with questions of legitimation, the second with questions of substance. To take the second track first, it should be said that much of the sort of "reading" that Spivak offers is indeed similar to and most likely influenced by the general approach to reading that de Man offers in many of his works, most clearly in the collection of essays that Spivak cites, *Allegories of Reading*. This affinity is not surprising, at least in part because in the mid-1960's Spivak was de Man's student at Cornell University (where he supervised her doctoral thesis, as the contributors notes to *Marxism and the Interpretation of Culture* remind us). Indeed, Spivak's championing of deconstruction's techniques and her adherence to deconstruction's philosophical tenets have been consistent throughout her best-known writings, from the lengthy critical introduction to her translation of Derrida's *Of Grammatology* (1976) onwards. True, the choice of the bedfellows de Man and Gramsci is surprising, especially because the sort of historical investigation that Gramsci advocates throughout all of his works, without exception, is precisely the sort of historical investigation that de Man, in a series of prefaces in the late 1970's, was at pains to repudiate in terms of his own views as expounded in his writings.[12] However (surprise again), the principal locus of de Man's statement of his rejection of historical approaches — that is, the rejection of the historical project that he describes his own work as setting out with, but which he would not or could not sustain — is found precisely at the beginning of the preface to *Allegories of Reading*:

Allegories of Reading started out as a historical study and ended up as a theory of reading. I began to read Rousseau seriously in preparation for a historical reflection on Romanticism and found myself unable to progress beyond local difficulties of interpretation. In trying to cope with this, I had to shift from historical definition to the problematics of reading.[13]

This passage, which, to repeat, is typical of de Man's later renunciations of what might be termed the sort of historical imperative that by contrast informs all of Gramsci's materialist readings and analyses, is especially instructive here, because it demonstrates the stretch of the imagination that is required by a writer like Spivak who would attempt to yoke together de Manian deconstruction and Gramscian historiography. In this instance, Spivak's critical mixture is utterly unsuccessful for the simple reason that the two orientations have nothing to do with each other beyond being irresolvably contrary one to another. (Happily, when a little later in that same preface de Man describes his reading of Rousseau as a sustained attempt at "the *elaboration* and the undoing of tropological transformations" [my italics], Spivak does *not* cast her net so widely as to pull in de Man's unhighlighted use of "elaboration" amidst the same catch in which she located, albeit by way of Said, Gramsci's equally unhighlighted use of the term.)

So much for the substance of the linked reference, a linking that, again, occurs implicitly in "Deconstructing Historiography" and explicitly, albeit via a footnote, in "Can the Subaltern Speak?" But if the *substance* of the reference is indeed so tenuous, even contradictory, how can the reference be explained? The answer, it seems to me, lies in consideration of the other track suggested above, that of the *legitimation* of critical/theoretical discourse, a track that in this case is itself dual. The first element here has to do with the fate of deconstruction in the academy, specifically in the rising tide of cultural studies, which in the mid-1980's, when Spivak's essays appeared, seemed ready to overwhelm deconstruction's previously dominant intellectual position. The conference "Marxism and the Interpretation of Culture" at the University of Illinois, in which Spivak delivered "Can the Subaltern Speak?," was held in the summer of 1983, a few months before Paul de Man's tragic death. "Deconstructing Historiography" was first published in *Subaltern Studies* in 1985. Both essays thus took shape in a period during which deconstruction was hard-pressed by competing lines of inquiry with very different critical/theoretical assumptions (pressed, but neither eclipsed nor vituperated as it was following the subsequent revelation of de Man's collaborationist writings of the 1930's and 1940's). What better way in the mid-1980's to legitimize the continuing use of de Manian deconstruction than by inserting that very discourse into the realm of cultural studies itself? And what better way to legitimize Spivak's own discourse, following the second element of this dual track, than by inserting that deconstructive reference by way of open citation of the then-current favorite of the proponents of cultural studies in the United States and England, Antonio Gramsci? That the first sort of legitimation had no bearing on reality and the second most likely had little relation to what Spivak actually knew, regardless of her seemingly authoritative reference to Gramsci's criticism as contained in "texts *such as* 'The Southern Question' " (my italics) — texts with which she would seem to have at best a passing acquaintance — appears, finally, to make no difference. The process of legitimation thus gives evidence, in this case, of being stronger than any concern for either historical substance or intellectual rigor. In other words, the one track, in its own duality, has effectively untracked the other. The totalizing impetus that set Spivak's doubly allusive critical machine in motion — the sort of impetus in which de Man's anti-totalizing attitude in his mature works would never have permitted him to indulge — has returned, upon investigation, to wreck the machine itself.

How could this have happened in the first place? In order to consider that question, it might be best to review once more the quotation from "Deconstructing Historiography" cited above. Several aspects of this quotation have already been treated, but at this point I would like to emphasize a particularly important part of what Spivak says, a part that has major implications for the entire project of cultural studies: "If seen in this way [i.e., from the supposedly Gramscian perspective of *elaborare*], the work of the Subaltern Studies group repeatedly makes it possible for us to grasp that the concept-metaphor of the 'social text' is not the reduction of real life to the page of a book." I do not intend to comment here either on Spivak's use of "to grasp" as a verb of understanding, a verb with a more than venerable lineage in Marxist writings that have a praxis orientation, or on her allusion to the "social text," an allusion filled with meaning owing not only to the neo-Marxist tradition but also to her own participation in the activities and the publications of the editorial group operating in and around the journal of the same name from the mid-1970's up until today. Rather, I mean to focus on the concluding section of these remarks, on Spivak's assertion that her interest in Gramscian analysis is due to the fact that once this perspective is adopted it is possible to see that sociocultural analysis, in the form of "transactional reading," is not the "reduction of real life to the page of a book." This is a position of genuine change for which I must declare a great deal of sympathy, and it is one with which, no doubt, Gramsci would have agreed, had he had any idea that something like "transactional reading" existed. The problem is the context of the affirmation. Let's retrace its background. First, Gramsci uses the term *elaborare* in the twofold sense we have discussed. Second, Said adopts the term within a somewhat different set of concerns, and in the process elides the surrounding paragraphs, which bristle with questions of bad faith, ideology, politics, popular philosophy, and the interrelation of common sense and "vulgar" or accepted ideas in the everyday world of sociopolitical engagement. Third, Spivak adopts the term in a context bereft of its Gramscian depth (though not of its Gramscian name tag), in service of a further, yet polemically — and in this context uncannily — ahistorical notion of reading proposed by Paul de Man. How could the arc of trajectory of any such series of references be aimed more obviously *away* from the world of matter and sense and more obviously *into* the "page[s] of a book," and into the pages of a thoroughly academic book at that?

Retracing this trajectory leads us back not only to Said but also to the initial problem with which we began, that is, the question of the difference between descriptive and programmatic analysis. At this juncture I should affirm the overriding imperative of this driving concern as opposed to the relatively minor importance of the question regarding Spivak's (or anyone else's) use of Gramsci in an academic sense. What I am primarily concerned with here is *not* the question of academic utilization and reference in the "old curmudgeon" school of scholarly standards but rather the entire question of the relation between cultural investigation and genuine social practice, a question that I believe is broached by Spivak in a way that is equally significant for the fact that it is unintentional. That Said uses Gramsci in a fashion that adopts the Gramscian text as a springboard for Said's own program of analysis (and in the process misconstrues the details if not the overall thrust of Gramsci's writings) is perhaps acceptable in a sociopolitical as well as an academic sense.[14] That Spivak uses Gramsci borrowed from Said *and* from Guha *and* as part of her own reading, as a sort of *senhal* at once referring to and covering over the work of Paul de Man, seems acceptable in neither of these senses. Yet what is obviously informing Spivak's discourse here is the desire to establish the sort of reference that will serve not only as analysis but also as program, not only as academic investigation but also as social project, which is finally to say not only as description but also as action. In short, the illusion in Spivak's text (an illusion much more severe than in Said's work) is that merely by describing things in the right way and in the midst of the right context of allusions, one is not only producing academic discourse but, somehow, also intervening in the everyday world of praxis all around us, not only *saying* something but also *doing* something.

The actual problem, of course, lies not so much in saying as in doing, and particularly in doing *what*. There is an obvious temptation at this point to denounce the use of Gramsci within these examples of cultural studies as the idealist creation of an escape hatch, the introduction into academic discourse of a type of reference not designed to foster a notion of genuine material praxis but serving rather to provide the illusion of radical chic that merely dresses its windows with calls to action, thus allowing academic discourse to continue on its merry way while avoiding real and programmatic connection — and here both adjectives are crucial — with the everyday world. But I do not intend to paint Gramscian elements in contemporary cultural studies with such a broad brush. True, the importation of Gramscian notions into cultural studies in the Anglo-American world has at times been uneven, but more often than not its procedures have been both principled and productive. Though Spivak's attempt at adopting Gramsci's notion of elaboration seems, in the end, more abusive than either genuinely transactional in a de Manian sense or elaborative in a Gramscian one, other recent thinkers have in the long run actually fared much better. Interestingly enough, these thinkers often lead us to hypotheses that are themselves elaborations of previous Marxist thought, crucial elaborations in a period like our own in which radical reconsideration of prior Marxist positions is essential to current materialist philosophy. I am thinking, for instance, of Stanley Aronowitz's often incomplete understanding of Gramsci's multivalent conceptions of intellectuals, cultural hegemony, and educational praxis — an incompleteness that shows up, for example, throughout Aronowitz's *The Crisis in Historical Materialism* and in his more recent essay "Postmodernism and Politics,"[15] but which, in a manner reminiscent of Said's use of Gramsci, does not keep Aronowitz from understanding Gramsci's general position or from deriving useful conclusions from those positions. I am also thinking of Tony Bennett's admonition, referred to previously, that it is time to move beyond the period of the "Gramscian problematic" as set forth within cultural studies, a problematic that could easily be expanded, even while retaining its historical specificity (and so, in truly Gramscian terms, its historical limitations) regardless of Bennett's doubts.[16] I am thinking, too, of Stuart Hall's powerful description of the role Gramscian thought played in what for cultural studies overall were the formative years in the crucible of the Centre for Contemporary Cultural Studies in Birmingham, England. Hall's description ends with his reservations about both bookish academics and the deconstructive assumptions of current cultural studies, his "nagging doubt that this overwhelming textualization of cultural studies' own discourses somehow constitutes power and politics as exclusively matters of language and textuality itself."[17] In the works of these writers and many more, Gramsci's thought lives on as a source of both reference and inspiration, a spur to any intellect that wishes to absorb it as well as to any spirit that wishes to surpass it.

This last citation from Stuart Hall's essay brings us back, by way of a more or less commodious vicus of recirculation, to the question of textuality, that is, in this context, to what Spivak terms the page of a book, and to Gramsci's own concern that the systematic philosophical self-analysis that he was proposing not be understood, in his words, in a "pedantic" sense ("nel senso pedantesco"). But his concern does not stop there. What he actually says about this sort of systematic analysis is that it should not be understood "in the *pedantic and academic* sense" ("nel senso *pedantesco e professorale* della parola," my italics). What is to be made of this second adjective, which is in reality a false cognate? Hoare and Smith, perhaps understandably given the requirements of literal denotative translation, render the phrase "pedantesco e professorale" as "pedantic and academic," thus giving the English a ring of redundancy, the sort of redundancy, indeed imprecision, that Gramsci is often accused of by even his most sympathetic Anglo-American readers. But though Gramsci's notebooks are voluminous, they are not, in their final version (that is, in Gramsci's final revisions of his notes, signaled in the critical edition by differing type size), either redundant or imprecise. What "professorale" adds to "pedantesco" in Gramsci's Italian is not "academic" but rather something like "ostentatious," "conceited," "self-centered," or, in the plain style of colloquial English, "stuck up." The part that "professorale" plays in Gramsci's warning thus has less to do with the academy as such than with egocentrism. What this warning is all about, then, is part of what I have been trying to suggest for cultural studies overall: not to get caught up in the forest of (pedantically allusive) details that occlude rather than facilitate vision, and at the same time, not to get trapped in the blind alley of egotism, in the obsessive self-reference that makes everything appear understandable only in relation to the self, or, in this arena, only in relation to the all-powerful theorist. It is perhaps in this sense that we should once more review, however skeptically, Spivak's concluding remarks following her comments on *elaborare*, on the "social text," and, finally, on the necessity of avoiding the "reduction of real life to the page of a book." What she says at the paragraph's conclusion is: "My theoretical intervention is a modest attempt to remind us of this."

I will, of course, have something more to say about Spivak's "modest attempt" in a moment, but before that I would like to say a few words about another question that begs to be addressed: why Gramsci? There are several threads to this question, some of which have already been drawn out (threads concerning the legitimation of sociocultural discourse) or at least suggested (those concerning Gramsci's prior usefulness in the Anglo-American tradition of cultural studies). But it might be appropriate here, nearing my own conclusion, to center on two more such threads: first, the aspects of Gramscian thought that may well be of ongoing import in the field of cultural studies and, second, what it is about Gramsci and his writings that permits theorists like Spivak to treat his work in the way she does (and what this very treatment has to say about cultural studies as regards both its strength *and* its potential weaknesses or dangers). Gramsci's continuing utility for cultural studies resides, it seems to me, in the extraordinary weight that he gives to culture in the analysis of social formations and in the way he construes the relation between culture, society, and politics as a relation of *reciprocity* rather than *derivation*, thus seeing culture as an active force directly affecting every other area of material existence rather than (as in traditional Marxist conceptions) a mechanistically dependent part of an obfuscating superstructure that serves only to hide the truly generative powers at the economic base. These Gramscian postulates (buttressed by many others), about which I will have more to say in subsequent chapters, avoid both the paralysis that at times afflicts Foucauldian analysis and the elitist assumptions that permeate the otherwise useful works of the Frankfurt school, and they give culture itself an importance that continues to distinguish cultural studies as an authentic area of investigation with a potentially self-aware and productively reciprocal relation to its objects of inquiry.

The next thread of the question "Why Gramsci?" leads to considerations that, in terms of cultural studies as a discipline, are somewhat less sanguine. This part of the question can perhaps be framed by setting it off against another question: Why Gramsci and not, for example, Sartre or Heidegger or even Russell or Peirce? The answer to this query seems to me, in its implications for the contemporary practice of cultural studies, fairly depressing, since it is contained in the fact that Gramsci is Italian and wrote in

Italian (that is, modern Italian as opposed to medieval or Renaissance Italian) rather than French or German or English or American: Gramsci, irrespective of his brilliance and his utility, is, first, marginal and, second, not easily checked. (To put this crudely but, I think, accurately, since Spivak herself did not bother to check the substance of her citation against the original, why would or could or should anybody else?) This is thus not a matter of "creative" error but really of simple arrogance. While this sort of attitude may well be widespread within many areas of academic study, it would appear that, if cultural studies has any claim to validity that is genuinely new and positive, that claim is grounded in the understanding of culture as a field that is not to be marginalized by the canonical assumptions of high/low, elite/common, rare/everyday that underlie the treatment of a nontranslated (or incompletely translated) and nonmainstream (as the mainstream is defined in the academy in the United States) thinker as being exotic and/or esoteric no matter how fundamentally important. This is a fancy way of saying that what Spivak has done in this instance is questionable both in its form and its substance, but on reflection, it is difficult to know if "questionable" or even "abusive" is really the right term or if "thoroughly objectionable" would not do better. It should be noted, moreover, that Spivak's characteristic use of Gramsci continues in her most recent work.[18]

To conclude we should return one final time to Said's quotation of Gramsci's notebooks. In that passage, Gramsci recommended a dual process of individual and sociohistorical (i.e., communal) elaborative analysis while warning against two dangers, that of pedantry and that of egocentrism. Whereas Gramsci's recommendations are especially germane to the present situation and practice of cultural studies, his warnings seem even more important. It is doubtless true that a certain degree of narcissism is required to get the program of any academic study afloat and under way (whether in writing, lecturing, or reading). But it seems equally clear that academic narcissism carried to the obsessional extreme of seeing the other exclusively in terms of the self — or, in this case, of Spivak's seeing Gramsci, *pace* her "modest" disclaimer, in the mirror of first Said and then de Man, and subsequently reproducing that gaze as authentic in her own work — represents the sort of critical/theoretical practice that, rather than forwarding the progress of the ship of cultural studies, may in the end sink it. And — as meek a conclusion as this may be — since I believe in *both* the descriptive concerns *and* the programmatic goals of cultural studies today, that result would be, to my mind, too bad. At any rate, my intent in the next section of this study is to look at the sociohistorical thinkers who I believe genuinely help in understanding the program of literary/ cultural reading that I would propose at this juncture in critical thought within (and without) the American academy.

PART TWO

THE HISTORICAL
IMAGINATION

5

Vico, Hercules, and the Lion

Figure and Ideology in the Scienza nuova

GIAMBATTISTA VICO'S INTEREST in the etymologies not only of words but also of imaginative figures or images is a salient feature of the *Scienza nuova* (*New Science*) from beginning to end.[1] In the book's introduction, "Idea dell'opera" ("Idea of the Work"), Vico sets forth the principles and the goals of his treatise by explaining the "allegorical engraving" that he used as the book's frontispiece. Vico explains the figure of the Lion in the frontispiece by reference both to the zodiac (in which it appears in the engraving) and to Hercules, whom, in Vichian logic, the Lion suggests, since it was Hercules who slew the Nemean Lion and wore the Lion's skin (par. 3). Vico then associates the Lion, which at its death vomited flames, with the great primordial forest that once covered the earth and that was burned down by the first human "Herculean" heroes, who thus established their political power through what became more or less stable communities tied to the local cultivation of the earth. Before moving from the figure of the Lion to that of Virgo (the other figure in Vico's zodiacal representation), Vico connects Hercules to the founding of the Olympics, as a festival celebrating Hercules' victory, as well as to the establishment of all Greek society based on agriculture; and he subsequently follows a similar process of explanation in regard to the sign of Virgo.

This explanatory procedure, here as elsewhere in Vico's work, consists first in describing or redescribing cultural images and then in decoding their meanings through successive layers of encoded historical signification. Accordingly, such "imaginative genera" as Aesop, Achilles, Prometheus, Polyphemus, Ulysses, Homer, and a host of others are seen as symbolic figures representing concrete moments in the first two stages of humankind's threefold development (from primitive, malformed beings wandering the primordial forest of the earth in solitude, to socially domesticated individuals ruled over first by political then by military heroes, and ultimately to free and individually responsible subjects living in the age of reason). Whereas mankind in the first two ages is given to constructing these naive but powerful poetic images through the successive tropes of metaphor, metonymy, and synecdoche, man in the third age, the age of rational reflection — which is the proper, final attainment of human nature — is, or should be, given not so much to the *creation* as to the *analysis* of such images. Analytic, potentially ironic reflection thus furnishes the means by which Vico reinterprets the history of the gentile nations (though, as we shall see, rational analysis does not in the end tell the whole story of Vico's project), and the figures of the Lion and the Virgin constitute the first proving ground for Vico's method.

The figure of the Virgin, Vico points out, is traditionally described by poets as being crowned with ears of grain because in poetic tradition the history of Greece began with the Golden Age, and, Vico asserts, grain was the first gold of the primitive world. Interpretation of the iconography of the figures of Hercules and Virgo thus demonstrates the socioeconomic basis of earliest human society; and (through Vico's further consideration of the Roman deity Saturn, who corresponds to the Greek god Cronus) it also shows the beginning of the reckoning of time by the regular cycles of games and harvests.

The distinctions between the gods and the heroes are apparent in Vico's remark that, in the imagination of primitive men, the gods were eventually raised to the planets and the heroes to the fixed stars, or constellations. But at this preliminary point in his discussion, Vico's intent is not so much to distinguish the human heroes from the gods (whom, through fear, mankind had created) as to assert the interaction of gods and heroes in the minds of the first men living in primitive society: "Nella qual età dell'oro pur ci dissero fedelmente i poeti che gli dèi in terra praticavano con gli eroi" ("In this age of gold, the poets assure us faithfully, the gods consorted on earth with the heroes," par. 3). Hercules thus becomes a crucial transitional figure, a human being yet also the son of Jove, half god and half man, the hero who ushered in the new age of the heroes and thus represented the starting point for all heroic civil society.

In treating these poetic figures, Vico's purpose is not, of course, to consider the figures or their iconography in and of themselves, through strictly rhetorical analysis, but instead to get at the historical truth that the figures *in toto* represent, through what might be termed a poetic hermeneutics of human history. Although the variants of the figure of Hercules are inevitably multiple ("si truova ogni nazione gentile antica narrarne uno, che la fondò" ["every gentile nation boasts one as its founder," par. 3]), the historical reality for which this figure stands is always the same: the transition from the most primitive familial groups, in which ancient men lived with their female partners in natural caverns, to heroic communal society based on agriculture. Indeed, the uniformity of human development is attested to all the more forcefully by the multiplicity of the versions of this heroic figure, since all variants, when interpreted correctly (which is to say in the Vichian manner) tell the identical story.

Later on in the *Scienza nuova*, therefore, when Vico interprets the myth of Cadmus, he finds it to be nothing other than a specifically Theban version of the story of Hercules (par. 679). Cadmus slays the dragon—which, for Vico, means clearing the earth of the primordial forest—and then sows the teeth in the ground (i.e., plows the first fields with curved pieces of wood). The heavy stone thrown by Cadmus in the myth stands for the hard earth that the dependent *famuli* wanted to plow themselves, and the armed men who sprang forth represent the fight between the now-united heroes and the plebeians in the revolt over the questions at issue in the first agrarian law. When Cadmus is himself changed into a serpent, this transformation represents the origin of the aristocratic senate's authority in both ancient Greek and ancient Latin society, and, through a marvelous Vichian conflation of the Athenian lawgiver Draco and the word "Dragone," or "Dragon," the writing out in blood of ancient Greek law. The stories of Hercules and of Cadmus thus indicate, for Vico, identical referents, the ordered, material development of ancient society over the course of "many centuries" (par. 679). It should be noted as well that this Vichian tale of mankind's historical progression includes not only generative historical creation and conflict but also, at transitional moments, typically Vichian notions of degeneration, as demonstrated in the myth of Hercules first by the hero's symbolic subjugation and feminization at the Lydian court of Queen Omphale and then by the bestial contamination of Hercules' blood through the agency of the centaur Nessus and the hero's resultant death (i.e., the social reforms giving rise to the intermixing of plebeian and heroic blood and the eventual dominance of the former over the latter).

Because in Vico's method investigation proceeds from concrete examples toward general principles, his historical "science" may seem both inductive and empirical, and to a certain extent this dual characterization of his approach is correct. In agreement with Bacon, and in opposition to what Vico considers the tradition of metaphysics leading up to and including Descartes, Vico intends a study not of "criticism" but of "topics," which will retrace and reinterpret ancient man's progressive development on the way to the establishment of modern society. In a key passage near the end of book 2 ("Poetic Wisdom"), shortly after the interpretation of the myth of Cadmus, Vico describes the two main "operations" of the mind, the first of which, roughly speaking inductive perception, is shaped by the "regulating art" of topics, while the second, deductive logic, is shaped by that of criticism (par. 699).

The opposition of reason and sense is not at all odd or new, and neither is the Aristotelian bias evident in Vico's insistence that sense is the primary component of the two (cf. Vico's earlier scholastic paraphrase of the Aristotelian dictum, "Nihil est in intellectu quin prius fuerit in sensu," par. 363). But for the overall project of the *Scienza nuova*, Vico's *historicization* of the opposition is telling indeed. That the art of topics, as the direct sensual perception of the surrounding world, implies induction and discovery is far from surprising, yet the other part of Vico's concept is fascinating, to say the least, since he also links topics to invention and to fantasy. Vico does this by way of the functions of memory: "Ma la fantasia altro non è che risalto di reminiscenze, e l'ingegno altro non è che lavoro d'intorno a cose che si ricordano" ("fantasy is nothing other than the springing up again of reminiscences, and ingenuity or invention is nothing other than the working over of what is remembered," par. 699). Topics — which, it should be emphasized, are the operational means by which the primitive mind works since rational reflection and critical deductive logic do not really develop until later — are thus linked both to the understanding of the world via direct perception of particulars and to the faculty of the imagination. This link explains the necessarily poetic perception and imitative poetic expression of the first men, whose fantasy was as passionately robust as their reasoning power was weak (cf. pars. 185, 215–19, 704, 825). In Vico's historical scheme, poetry therefore comes of necessity *before* prose (and he notes that Memory, as Mnemosyne, was considered, and rightly so, as the mother of the Muses), which is why for Vichian historiography the study of philology, of poetic particulars, is the first step, and the study of philosophy, or critically examined general propositions (cf. pars. 138–40, 819–21), comes only later.

This division between topics and criticism within Vichian thought reflects another, that between the "certain" evidence of particular details and events and the "true" general patterns that such evidence eventually comes to suggest. Philology, as the study of individual entries in early man's "mental dictionary," thus examines certain, specific evidence that will lead to a communal truth concerning *all* the primitive languages of the gentile nations (par. 35 et passim). Since the order of ideas, which is to say the development of the human mind, must proceed according to the order of things, or the material progression of human history (par. 238), the proper method in retracing gentile human history is to start at the beginning (i.e., the great Flood) and to move forward following early man's movement in the time when he knew only "the certain," as consciousness (*coscienza*), and *not* "the true," as science (*scienza*), which is to say, as consciousness *plus* reason, or full human knowledge.

In interpretative terms, the figural springboard for Vico's treatise is thus the empirical realm of conflict and change that gave rise to the modification of the human mind as history progressed (pars. 331, 374). Marx was correct, then, in *Capital* (1, 4, 15, 1) to express his admiration for Vico's refusal to dwell on the mystifying preoccupations of metaphysics and for Vico's steadfast attention to the history of the world as man had made that history (i.e., the well-known Vichian formula — using another sense of *vero* — *verum ipsum factum*, "what is true is what has been made [by man]"). In accordance with the *Scienza nuova*'s program, Vico regards the poetic figures with which we began here *not* as analogical or philosophical allegories (as other philosophers of Vico's time had claimed, and particularly the northern European proponents of Natural Law) but instead, when correctly understood, as univocal and historical allegories. In other words, such figures as Hercules and Cadmus do without doubt have a story to tell, but their stories are direct and true embodiments of primitive perceptions, not intentionally masked, clever allusions either to esoteric wisdom or to highly rational universal truths retold in figural form (which is to say, both the mode of and the appropriate interpretative procedures for these figures are precisely opposite those of the "allegorical engraving" that Vico himself offered as the starting point for the *Scienza nuova*).

Vico's analysis of cultural figures remains of interest today in various respects. For one thing, his conception of culture as the privileged locus of historical evidence goes against the classical Marxian notion of a clear distinction between a generating economic base and a static or passively reflective (at best secondary, at worst obfuscating) cultural superstructure. In Vico's analysis, language and cultural forms mix with economic, political, and social organization in a much more active and more compelling way than they do in standard reflection theory. At the same time, the Althusserian scheme of parallel realms of development, in which culture has its own generating infrastructure, is inadequate to account for the intertwining dynamics of the Vichian mixture of realms. Consideration of Althusser is useful in one respect, however, since it helps us move from questions of history as bits of evidence to a typically Vichian concern for the totality of historical evidence itself as made up of both human perception and human expression in time. This totality is indicative, therefore, of a unified historical situation *and* a worldview, which is to say of the (however conscious or unconscious) perception of human history, or, finally, of ideology. It is true that the unified nature of Vichian social development is itself not historically simple but complex, since, as Vico points out in a striking passage, the origins of all three types of society (of gods, heroes, and men) and all three types of thought and language (mute, mixed, articulated) dovetail in specific instances rather than being completely separate (par. 446), so that Vico's historical progression is really more a spiral than a line, with a special degenerative twist at the end in the form of the "recourses." And it is also true that speech as *language* — what Vico terms, in his summary at the end of book 4, the midpoint between the mind and the body — is the richest source of evidence in tracing the dynamics of mankind's development. It would, nonetheless, be misleading to stop here with these observations, since neither the materialist slant of Vico's economic and sociopolitical investigations nor the inductive cast of his linguistic examinations is really the entire aim of the *Scienza nuova.*

The other part of the book's aim, as Vico asserts again and again throughout his treatise in a wide variety of contexts, goes beyond the study of the temporal particulars of human history in all their mental and material modifications toward, eventually, consideration of history's universal, atemporal *truth*, which can be summed up in a phrase: providential order. Providence, in this context, should be understood as an immanent mechanism for ordered development. In other words, what is important here is the question of Providence's orderly system of worldly effects, not the question of its putative transcendent source. This is, after all, consonant with Vico's own emphasis. As Bruce Haddock has commented: "Though [Vico] refers repeatedly to God's eternal order, his principal concern throughout the *Scienza nuova* is not to give a rational justification of God's plan but rather to account for the order which can be discerned in the emerging customs of men. Vico thus . . . focuses his attention on the immanent operation of providence in historical development."[2]

As Haddock notes, this combination of interests in man as *homo faber* and in Providence as orderly force gives the *Scienza nuova* its peculiar flavor. For Vico, the remarkably uniform patterns of repetition in the development of all the gentile nations (i.e., those not benefited by the revelation afforded the Hebrews) attests to the guiding force of Providence. To put this in other terms, man made the world in specific time and material particulars, but Providence ordered the making of its institutions following laws that are universal and eternal (par. 342). That all primitive societies shared the three principal institutions of burial, matrimony, and religion, that they all followed the same principal stages of social, economic, and political development, and that all men follow identical psychic development (feeling, perception, and reflection, in which, as for Freud, Vichian ontogeny in its last era repeats phylogeny) make manifest the unifying, orderly effects of providential force. The polemically antidiffusionist stance taken throughout the *Scienza nuova* is thus not just an aspect of Vico's sense of anthropology but, more to the point, of his own philosophical belief. I have commented elsewhere on the worldly effects of Providence's workings and on Providence's relation to human knowledge and human freedom in Vichian thought.[3] Suffice it here first to reaffirm, along with Vico, the aim of his work, the discovery of true historical identity amidst seeming difference so that "we will have the ideal history of the eternal laws," and then to repeat the boast of the work's author, who has composed a study of "the certain" and thus also, implicitly, of "the true," of philology *and* philosophy, of particular *coscienza* that leads to universal *scienza*:

Laonde non potemmo noi far a meno di non dar a quest'opera l'invidioso titolo di *Scienza nuova*, perch'era un troppo ingiustamente defraudarla di suo diritto e ragione, ch'aveva sopra un argomento universale quanto lo è d'intorno alla natura comune delle nazioni, per quella propietà c'ha ogni scienza perfetta nella sua idea.

Hence we could not refrain from giving this work the invidious title of a *New Science*, for it was too much to defraud it unjustly of the rightful claim it had over an argument so universal as that concerning the common nature of nations, in virtue of that property which belongs to every science that is perfect in its idea. (par. 1096)

"Perfect in its idea": no phrase could be more telling in regard to Vico's estimation of the extraordinary import of his project, which consists in nothing less than the rational understanding of Providence through examination of its empirical, worldly effects, which is to say, as Vico comments at the very beginning of his book, in constructing for the first time "una teologia civile ragionata della provvedenza divina" ("a rational civil theology of divine providence," par. 2). The all-encompassing nature of Vico's program thus derives from his intent to find the basic similarity amidst apparently disparate events and to approach thereby the knowledge of Providence conceived of as "una divina mente legislatrice" ("a divine legislative mind," par. 133), a force capable of turning human vices into human virtues, thoroughly individual self-love into society organized for the common good, concrete human particulars into the (providentially shaped) totality of progressive human history.

The "imaginative genera" of the figures of poetic language, which constitute the locus in which language, myth, and history come together, thus represent the worldview, or again, the ideology, of particular moments in historical development, moments the true meaning of which can only be understood, however, *a posteriori*, as part of the uniform progression guided by providential force. The workings of Providence are immanent but indirect. Vico therefore escapes the notion of innate ideas, a model of uniform human nature so tempting as to have beguiled such recent psychological, social, and aesthetic thinkers as Carl Jung, Northrop Frye, and, to a certain extent, Noam Chomsky, by positing a guardian of human development that is internally efficient yet also externally valid. Moreover, rather than searching for the totalizing "one myth" that would demonstrate the innately uniform organization of the human mind—as, for example, in the project of Lévi-Strauss—Vico continually searches for the "one (hi)story," which is indeed the story of man's internal and external development but only as that story is told and retold in *countless* myths through providential agency. With both his predecessors and his successors, Vico thus enjoys a relationship of significant similarity as well as difference. In anticipation of a Girardian notion of sacrificial order but with no clear sense of victimage, of a Foucauldian esteem for cultural evidence but with no demonstrable concern for contemporary examples, Vico places Cartesian subjectivism and Renaissance analogizing thought in the balance of historical truth and finds each of them wanting. Vico's intention is, of course, to create a type of science that is at once both literally "new" and correct. By starting with what he considers to be the concrete evidence of philology, Vico means to pass beyond both the individual subject *and* material proofs to arrive at the abstract meaning of philosophy, in the rational mode of investigation that is ultimately characteristic of the human mind in its highest state of development.

But however confident and/or enticing Vico's new science may appear, it is nevertheless important to see that there are two major ways in which the programmatic rigor of the inductive/empirical claim of his own methodology is undercut, or, better, undercuts itself, all along. One of these ways has to do with Vico's own worldly sense of religious philosophy (as an understanding of the workings of Providence, not as a function of the Church) and the other with Vico as, broadly stated, a poet. Both have to do with the author's own worldview, with the ideology not only of the poetic/historical objects of his discourse but also with the object of the *Scienza nuova*'s discursive subject, Vico himself; and both have to do with Vico's constant concern for locating order amidst what may otherwise seem nothing but randomness.

It is probably impossible to read the *Scienza nuova* without noting Vico's concern for—indeed, obsession with—ordered systems. Vico begins, as the *Scienza nuova*'s polemic dictates, with the concrete historical particulars of human development, with the specific "poetic" truths of human history. But at each stage of his own discourse, he insists on the uniform order to be found in the world (an order the perception of which is inherently pleasing to man [par. 204]), and he takes special care to provide order for his own discourse. This is not to say that the seemingly endless rounds of threes, the occasional flurries of attentively numbered asseverations, and the elaborate self-explanations casting backward as well as forward actually make the *Scienza nuova* a simple or unified text. Indeed, the *disorder* that the totalizing anxiety for order can perceive but cannot finally dominate attests to the generic status of Vico's work as what Frye would term an encyclopedic text (and it is germane in this context to recall that it was the Joyce of *Finnegans Wake* who regarded Vico as one of his own project's most authentic predecessors). The consistency and the truth of Vico's study are secured, nonetheless, by its combination of interests — by its mirroring of the apparent disorder of the world in reproducing the world's evidence *and* by its attempt to begin to put that evidence in order and thus to approach a knowledge of the providential effects that already exist within the world's story. The Vichian rage for order thus stands as nothing other than the genuine desire for unified, ordered systems, again construed in providential terms, and it is in this sense that the *Scienza nuova*'s remarkable final period should be read like the traditional epigram of the fable, half appropriate and half out of place: "Insomma, da tutto ciò che si è in quest'opera ragionata è da finalmente conchiudersi che questa Scienza porta *indivisibilmente seco* lo studio della pietà, e che, se non siesi pio, non si può daddovero esser saggio" ("To sum up, from all that we have set forth in this work, it is to be finally concluded that this Science carries *indivisibly with it* the study of piety, and that he who is not pious cannot be truly wise," par. 1112, my italics).

Vico's treatise thus provides an approach to the knowledge of providential order (heretofore barred from the human intellect) not only through the objects of its study but also through the form of its own discourse. The rational order that exists from the beginning of the *Scienza nuova*'s examination of particulars is thus buttressed by the workings of an overarching, ordered system of philosophical/historical belief, this, too, from the outset. At the same time, Vico the scientist is paired with Vico the poet. This is true not only in the methodological sense that we have noted — that Vico's study is of necessity, at least at its start, concerned with topics as distinguished from criticism — but also, once more in terms of Vico's own discourse, in the form of his metaphorization of his work. (To give just one early example, from the opening of the section "Elements" in book 1: "i seguenti assiomi o degnità . . . come per lo corpo animato il sangue, così deono per entro scorrervi ed animarla in tutto ciò che questa Scienza ragiona"; "these [elements] . . . just as the blood does in animal bodies, will course through our Science and animate it in all its reasonings," par. 119.) Here as elsewhere, from the very first pages of the *Scienza nuova*, the poet blends with the scientist, the philologist with the philosopher, in forging the ideologically and poetically ordered worldview that is found at the heart of Vico's object of investigation and that, in another guise, determines the form of Vico's discourse.[4] As distinct from his objects of study, however, Vico possesses the worldview that can exist only in the age of rational reflection and only with the aid not just of Providence but also of the human understanding of Providence, the one certain *and* true worldly force. The *Scienza nuova* thus takes its final shape as the book of the world *and* the book of the science of the world, Vico's ideologically motivated and ideologically framed study of historical figure and historical ideology as they are found at work in the best story imaginable, the one told and retold in Providence's worldly volume.

6

Hayden White's *The Content of the Form*

A Vichian View

THAT VICO'S THOUGHT had an extraordinary impact on the historical conception and the theoretical formulation of Hayden White's early works is no secret.[1] In *Metahistory* (1971) as well as in *Tropics of Discourse* (1978), the importance of Vico is obvious both from White's repeated allusions to the *Scienza nuova* and from his extended discussions of Vico's historical schemas. With the appearance of the collection of White's essays entitled *The Content of the Form*, it might seem that the "Vichian moment" of White's intellectual development has passed, since the collection not only lacks substantive discussion of Vico but also fails to demonstrate any reference whatever to his works.[2] To take this tack in coming to terms with White's corpus, however, would be thoroughly misleading since, despite the absence of direct reference, White's writings continue to give evidence of the pervasive influence of Vico's thought on the way that White himself imagines the historical enterprise in today's academic, cultural, and social environment. To put this in different terms, it seems to me that Vico figures in White's collection in much the same way that Nature and the Universe figured in Jorge Luis Borges's account of the metaphysicians' view of the world's sphere, which was so astonishing precisely because its outlines were so elusive, a fearful sphere, "whose center is everywhere and whose circumference is nowhere."[3]

What are the indications of this Vichian presence? One of them is to be found in White's insistence on the significance of the material fact of historical inquiry's object. Although White is pointedly attentive to the *textuality* of all historical discourse, he is also aware that, even though we have access to historical materials only through the "textual readings" fundamental to human perception, this does not mean that there is nothing that exists *outside* of textuality. Indeed, it is White's belief in the material fact of sociohistorical evidence that sets him at odds with the ahistorical, idealist approach of structuralist and (some) poststructuralist analyses, as he explains in a 1983 essay on Vico's similarities to and divergences from these recent philosophical trends, with special reference to the works of Lévi-Strauss, the early Roland Barthes, Jacques Lacan, Michel Foucault, Jacques Derrida, Julia Kristeva, and Philippe Sollers.[4]

But if White is implicitly averse to the antihistorical, often nihilistic slants of such examples of post-Nietzschean thought, he is equally opposed — again in Vichian fashion — to the linear recounting of historical "fact" in a naively mechanistic or positivistic manner. The value that White places on the *imaginative* faculty of the historian's perspective in the re-creation of the generative dynamics of historical truth is evident throughout the lively discussions of *The Content of the Form*, and it is this turn of mind, materially oriented yet thoroughly creative, that places White in opposition not only to the idealist mystifications of Parisian and Anglo-American structuralism but also to the ingenuously nondialectical empiricist trap of current neopositive intellectual programs. This cast of White's thought is clearest in his mid-1970's review of Leon Pompa's treatment of Vico, in which the imaginative thrust of Vico's "science" is valued in its own right, but its effects are also discernible throughout *The Content of the Form*.[5] A true descendant of Vico, White thus utilizes the best of both structuralist and neopositivist thought even as he swims against the tide of each of them. This is far from a simple procedure, however, since in the process White stakes out his own ground in a region contiguous to these and other contemporary schools but coterminous with none of them.

White's collection opens with three essays treating various interrelated questions of historiography and narrative theory, and it then proceeds with more practical discussion of these same issues through five chapters offering detailed readings of specific authors (J. G. Droysen, Foucault, Fredric Jameson, Paul Ricoeur, and, in the course of a practical/theoretical conclusion, Henry Adams). Throughout, one of the principal topics of the book, and no doubt one of those by which *The Content of the Form*, both as historiography and as general theory, must in the end stand or fall, is the nature and function of narrative discourse. White's notion of narrativity as the imposition of narrative order on the inherently nonordered materials of social history explains his assertion — correct, in my view — that narrative constitutes not so much a genre as a mode of discourse. Borrowing the shorthand of Jameson (who in turn had borrowed it from Louis Hjelmslev), White shows that narrative as such is not "neutral," as many bourgeois historians would insist, but that narrative's very form of unified, comprehensible "story" already has its own content from the outset (be this "time," as for Ricoeur, "the political," as for Jameson, "power," as for Foucault, and so forth). This concept of narrative as a form that is also a special mode of presentation, one that gives shape to the random "stuff" of the world, provides White with a means of addressing the basic question to which he and so many other theorists in the humanities have been drawn in recent years, the question of ideology. That White does so without condemning narrativity itself, as the *Annales* school would, for example, seems especially significant to me. But order is not the only aspect of narrativity on which White focuses his attention. The other key aspect — and here White is not far from Vico's idea of the continuing historical power of metaphor and Vico's consequent fascination with etymology — is that of the residual force, or, better, the encoded vitality of narrative as discursive metaphor. This interest on White's part is perhaps clearest in his chapters on Droysen and Jameson, but it runs throughout White's text and represents, *in toto*, one of the salient indications of White's ongoing affinity with Vichian thought. This combination of formal and ethical (or moral) concerns in *The Content of the Form* has been discussed in various contexts, but its Vichian roots have not, as yet, been accorded the acknowledgment they deserve.[6]

One of the outgrowths of these meditations on narrative history, that of the very possibility of writing "poststructuralist" history, might at first glance seem germane primarily to the academic discipline of history itself, but I believe that in the long run its implications are much broader than this, extending as they do throughout all humanistic studies. According to the line of argumentation in White's well-known essay on Jameson, originally published in *Diacritics* in 1982 and now revised and expanded in *The Content of the Form*, the challenge afforded to present historiography is to find not a genuine way back into (typically nineteenth-century) notions of history and logical narrativity but a way out of them altogether. In White's words, evocative both of Jameson's concerns and of those expressed by Joyce's Stephen Dedalus, "The problem may be not how to get into history but how to get out of it."[7] However, despite White's genuinely stimulating appeal (voiced from his preface onward) at the very least to conceive of a nontraditionally narrativized postmodern and poststructuralist history, it is nowhere clear just what that sort of history would be like.

To take this next step is perhaps too much to ask from a book that already offers a great deal in terms of both theoretical speculation and practical analysis, but such a consideration does lead, however circuitously, to the last point of this Vichian *riassunto* or summary. This point has to do with speculation as well as analysis and with intellectual commitment as well as investigation. By the time of the definitive version of the *Scienza nuova*, Vico had settled on a historical scheme and a historical method, to each of which his allegiance was passionate, even obsessive. This is not, of course, the only way to work and write, but Vico's demonstration of intellectual commitment seems to me to furnish a lesson of particular moment in today's critical climate, which is to say among the welter of positions and counterpositions taken, and all too often fudged, in the name of something that can be called theory: historical, literary, philosophical, cultural, and so on. White's book is challenging and convincing as far as it goes, and its opening and closing calls for new protocols and new assumptions in contemporary historiography are undeniably suggestive. But is it enough today to be merely suggestive? Vico's lesson, it seems to me, was otherwise. But maybe it is precisely on this terrain that White really has parted company with the master. To ascertain whether this is the case — and, if so, whether for good or for ill — will now require awaiting White's further investigations: all in all an engaging and exciting prospect.

7

Yesterday, Today, Tomorrow

Notes on Antonio Gramsci's Theory
of Literature and Culture

IN THE ARENA OF literary and cultural theory, Antonio Gramsci's primary contributions concern the historical evaluation of culture, and in particular the crucial social role that culture is seen to play when construed from Gramsci's distinctively post-Marxian, early-twentieth-century perspective. Gramsci published a great amount of material before the period of his incarceration in the mid-1920's, primarily articles written for the newspapers and journals with which he was associated in Turin, such as *L'Ordine Nuovo* and *Avanti!*, and there do exist significant differences between his early and later thought (especially in regard to Benedetto Croce's influence and to Gramsci's view of Italy as a backward or an advanced economic society). But the lasting contribution of Gramsci's sociopolitical and cultural writings is constituted by the massive collection *Quaderni del carcere* (*Prison Notebooks*), the roughly thirty notebooks written between 1919 and 1935; and for the most part it is on the basis of this body of work that Gramsci's theoretical contribution should be assessed.[1]

Gramsci conceives of both literature within culture and culture within society in terms of his characteristic set of sociopolitical categories: hegemony, ideology, and the division between civil society and political society. From Gramsci's point of view, culture does not function as a mere reflection of the economic base; but if culture is not regarded as utterly contingent, neither is it envisioned as being a totally separate entity with its own integral group of mediating base-superstructure relations, as is the case in some competing social analyses. While it is important to note that Gramsci thus rejects both standard Marxist reflection theory (explicit in Georgi Plekhanov, implicit in much of Georg Lukács and Lucien Goldmann) and the Althusserian sort of mystification at work in current theories of parallel realms, it is equally necessary to point out that Gramsci never abandoned the Marxian infrastructure-superstructure schema. Rather, he recast the underlying notion of reflection, in which the vital economic base generates its masked and/or obfuscating reflective superstructure, by changing the nature of the relationship from one of reflection to one of reciprocity. This formulation is at once traditional and innovative, retaining the usual Marxist concern for economics while avoiding the sort of narrow "economismo" attributed incorrectly to Marxism by Croce and furnishing an additional dynamic in the genuinely creative activity of cultural production. It is thus this theoretical conception of mutually reciprocal forces that gives culture its authentic power in Gramsci's thought even as his thought retains, *grosso modo*, the traditional Marxist framework.

This assessment of the overall significance that Gramsci's work holds for literary and cultural theory should be complemented by consideration of two somewhat more specific issues, Gramsci's rigorous historicism and his concern for popular — as opposed to elite — culture. In its openly historicist slant, Gramsci's work demonstrates his penchant for adopting other thinkers' critical categories and terminology (in this regard, those of Vincenzo Cuoco, Croce, Georges Sorel, and Lenin) as well as his eventual reworking of these prior concepts to his own ends. Gramsci's interest in cultural history also encompasses the history of folklore, as the cultural expression of Italy's subaltern classes, and it does so in such a forthright way that Gramsci may be seen as the modern father of the sociology of literature and culture in Italy. This combination of

popular and historical studies is evident, too, in Gramsci's examination of the phenomenon of national-popular literature, which,
in modern Italy, he finds signally lacking. The reasons for this lack
are multiple. First, the absence of sociocultural unity at the popular
level, due on the one hand to the division between north and south
and the further fragmentation into strictly regional cultural organization, and on the other hand to the linguistic barriers created and
perpetuated by the maze of regional and local dialects. One possible solution to this sort of pervasive fragmentation could, of
course, be provided by higher forms of literary expression that
would attempt to recast local sociocultural concerns in a truly
national literary framework. But in Italy, according to Gramsci, the
nineteenth-century writers who attempted to create this fusion,
whether before or after Italy's Risorgimento, or "passive revolution," failed miserably (Alessandro Manzoni and Giovanni Verga,
for example, as opposed to the Russian success of Lev Tolstoi).

   In broad terms, Gramsci's concept of the process of domination
and oppression within human society, including cultural factors, is
complex but consistent. A social class dominates by attaining hegemony in civil as well as in political society, through the multi-
layered construction of a *blocco storico*, or "historical block," of
social power (a concept that Gramsci borrowed from Sorel and
retooled to suit the purposes of his own analysis). The dominating
class — often made up of historically contingent alliances, such as
that between the aristocracy and the Church in Gramsci's own
region of southern Italy — actively diffuses its ideologically motivated view of human society; but it is important to see that in
Gramsci's estimation ideology is not so much false consciousness
as a distorted vision of what is in fact the historical truth of a
particular social situation. Ideology, whether expressed in elite
forms or in political orations, sermons from the pulpit, or such
popular literary forms as song and folklore, is thus construed as
being an object of interpretation and understanding rather than of
denigration. For Gramsci as for Vico, the popular expression of
what Gramsci terms "common sense" contains a core of truth,
even though that truth has been subject, to a greater or lesser extent, to the distorting ideological forces of the dominant social

class. It is this core of truth, expressed by *all* men in their capacity (willy-nilly) as philosophers, that must be analyzed in the overall picture of historical investigation by the intellectuals of the present and future. Indeed, one of the tasks of "the philosophy of praxis" (the term Gramsci adopted in his notebooks for historical materialism, in part to avoid the watchful eye of the prison censors) is to explain both the roots and the ramifications of the historical development of currently operative ideologies.

It is at this point that literature enters most directly into the Gramscian framework. As acts of social expression, at once individual and communal, the various forms of literature play a unique role — distinct even from the roles of other arts — in the struggle for hegemony that makes up each modern society. On a different plane, criticism, too, can be seen to join in this struggle either explicitly or implicitly, through idealist evasion (as in the writings of Croce) or through attempted sociocultural engagement (as in the work of one of the often-acknowledged models for Gramsci's own critical practice, Francesco De Sanctis). In the more advanced countries of the West, in which social revolutions will most likely come from a gradual and thoroughgoing "war of position" rather than from a violent and immediate "war of movement," culture in general and literature in particular can come to play a key role both in countering existing hegemonies and in establishing new ones. This is true in Gramsci's thought not only because of the notion of reciprocity between base and superstructure discussed earlier but also because of Gramsci's genuine respect for the power of culture — and for the *potential* future benefits offered by the revolutionary contributions of "organic-collective" intellectuals — in all human endeavors.

At times in the notebooks, Gramsci's analysis of individual authors and their works becomes very detailed. Despite this closer focus, however, Gramsci's characteristic view of literary expression as a creative act, as a form of voluntary praxis, remains unchanged. The forces of hegemony are in various ways the historical objects of fictional representation, but with greater or lesser degrees of awareness in each separate work. Gramsci repeatedly castigates those writers (the many offspring of Padre Bresciani, an author singled out for attack by De Sanctis) who in attempting to represent the truth of everyday life only manage to reproduce their own socioreligious and cultural prejudices, which is to say, most often those of the Church and the dominant bourgeoisie. In a different vein, Gramsci's ambivalence concerning Luigi Pirandello's works carries over from Gramsci's earlier writings, though in the notebooks Pirandello is lauded for introducing the shock of dialectics into the theater and for being at one and the same time Sicilian, Italian, *and* European. Dante, too, though even more so, is the object of extended admiring discussion, in Gramsci's well-known treatment of Canto X of the *Inferno*. The futurists, on the other hand, are treated with an acerbity bordering on disdain, primarily for their immaturity and distinctly non-national/popular character. There are also, dispersed here and there, commentaries on the characteristics of other arts (the "collective" nature of architecture, the immediate force of music) and on the future of Italian literature (which, to fulfill its potential, must set its roots in what Gramsci terms the rich "humus della cultura popolare").[2] Of all Gramsci's comments on art, however, perhaps the most fascinatingly suggestive, given the period in which he wrote, are contained in those few passages in which he links the immediate *and* collective effects of music and oratory with, first, the theater, as melodrama, and second, the cinema, as, at least *in potentia*, the genuine *romanzo popolare* of the West's cultural future.[3]

The writings contained in Gramsci's prison notebooks were not widely diffused until well after the fall of Italian fascism. Initial arrangements to smuggle the notebooks out of Italy following Gramsci's death were made in 1937 by Gramsci's sister-in-law, Tatjana Schucht, yet they did not arrive in Moscow until almost exactly a year later. At roughly the same time, Palmiro Togliatti received copies to read while in exile in Spain. But owing in part to the massive editorial enterprise required to prepare Gramsci's writings for publication, the works written during the period of his incarceration did not begin to appear until the late 1940's, the letters in 1947, and the notebooks in 1948, published by Einaudi.

Since their publication, the principal controversy surrounding Gramsci's prison works has been whether or not his thinking is truly revolutionary in a strict Marxian sense. The various approaches to this question over the decades following the 1940's have often reflected internal divisions within the Italian Communist Party as well as within the Italian Left overall. Before turning to the reception of Gramsci's work, however, it is useful to recall that several notable political events set the stage for the appearance and reception of the *Quaderni*. First among these was the Communist Party's 1944 "svolta di Salerno," in which it was decided that the Party, under Togliatti's direction, would attempt to work together with the established political elements of postfascist Italy rather than aiming for an immediate and total violent revolution. This co-operative spirit did not, however, lead to successful long-term results, as was demonstrated by the exclusion of Communist participation in the postwar government in 1947–48, following Alcide De Gasperi's trip to the United States and the decision on the part of the moderate and conservative parties — and in particular the Christian Democrats — to govern the country without direct support or counsel from the Left. To complicate matters further, the Soviet Union's mid-1950's policy of de-Stalinization and the untoward invasion of Hungary in 1956 split the Italian Communist Party from the inside, with many of the Party's better-known artist-intellectuals jumping from what they regarded (and the metaphor is Italo Calvino's) as a rapidly sinking ship unfortunately modeled on the design of the antihumanist and anti-imaginative totalitarian regime in the Soviet Union.

For Italian writers the questions at stake had to do, in a truly Gramscian sense, with the place and the power of culture in contemporary society — that is, whether culture merely reflects society, whether it goes hand in hand with social change, or whether, and in what fashion, it actually instigates change. True, these same concerns had lain at the heart of the mid and late 1940's debates between Togliatti and Elio Vittorini carried on in the pages of *Rinascita* and *Il Politecnico*. But following 1956, these sorts of disagreements took on a more pressing aspect in Italy and, indeed, throughout Western Europe; and they eventually resurfaced, though in somewhat modified form, in the debates inside the avant-garde group of Italian writers that met for the first time in

Palermo in the early 1960's and that was quickly christened the "Gruppo 63." But despite continuing interest during these years in the relation between society and culture, Gramsci's thoughts on these issues did not receive full and open acknowledgment in the scholarly writings of postwar Italy until two occurrences of the mid-1960's: the appearance of Alberto Asor Rosa's landmark study of 1965, *Scrittori e popolo*,[4] and the international conference dedicated to the discussion of Gramsci's works held under the auspices of the University of Cagliari in Sardinia in April 1967, subsequently published as *Gramsci e la cultura contemporanea (Gramsci and Contemporary Culture)* in 1969.[5]

This was the second such conference on Gramsci's works, the first having been held in Rome in 1958. Since the Cagliari conference, as the title of the published acta suggests, dealt directly with the issues of culture and contemporary society, its results were at once more focused and more germane to this aspect of Gramsci's thought. It is true that the slant of many of the sessions at Cagliari, when viewed within the postwar history of the Italian Communist Party, tended to reflect the more conservative elements of the Party's intellectual leadership; but it is difficult to say to what extent, if any, this bias vitiated the conference's contribution to Gramsci studies in general. At any rate the conference as a whole provided a positive response to what remained for many on the Left the central, twofold question in contemporary Italian sociopolitical life: is real social change possible beginning with civil society rather than political society, and if so, can culture play an influential role in eventually achieving a new and truly just "stateless" version of social life *without* recourse to violent revolution?

These questions were addressed most directly in an often-discussed contribution by Norberto Bobbio,[6] but they show up in one form or another in almost all of the papers delivered at the conference. Gramsci's concept of the gradual but thoroughgoing "war of position" in the Left's attacks on the entrenched forces of advanced bourgeois capitalism — with intellectuals as well as workers playing crucial roles in shifting the weight of cultural/ideological hegemony within and without the contemporary bourgeois *blocco storico* — is sounded in various keys throughout the conference's proceedings. In this light, it is interesting, if not unproblematic, to recall the conference's date, thirty years following Gramsci's demise and, perhaps even more significantly, almost exactly one year prior to the momentous events of the spring of 1968.

The Cagliari conference also included papers dealing with more specifically literary issues. Natalino Sapegno's "Gramsci e i problemi della letteratura" ("Gramsci and the Problems of Literature") was the first of these.[7] In the course of his presentation of Gramsci's principal literary concerns, Sapegno made a pair of especially timely points. First, despite Gramsci's extraordinary perspicacity regarding literary topics, Gramsci was not a literary critic as such; rather, he saw literature as only a part — although a major one — of his overriding concerns, which were constituted first to last by questions of economic organization, political justice, and social truth. Second, in terms of the literary dialectic of form and content (concepts adopted by Gramsci from Croce, though put to new and different uses), Gramsci's characteristic interest was in literary content, often at the expense of literary form.

This latter point was much debated, beginning with the responses of fellow literary critics who were present at the conference itself. Indeed, Gramsci's attention (or lack of it) to questions of literary form was an issue implicitly at stake in one of the most significant post-Gramscian literary debates of the subsequent decade, initiated by Carlo Salinari's polemical restatement of Gramsci's critique of Manzoni's great nineteenth-century novel, *I Promessi Sposi (The Betrothed)*.[8] In this essay of 1974, Salinari emphasized Gramsci's comments on such literary issues as perspective, humor, and irony in Manzoni's distanced and often patently aristocratic view of the novel's lower-class characters, the *gente meccaniche* that provide *I Promessi Sposi* with its story as well as its sociocultural background. Although the substance of Salinari's treatment drew later attacks (most tellingly from Sebastiano Timpanaro), Salinari's readjustment of critical emphasis in considering Gramsci's interest in literary form as well as in content was of undeniable importance.[9] Another set of papers at the Cagliari conference served to fill out Gramsci's literary concerns, those dedicated to Gramsci's conception of literature not only in its elite forms but also in its more popular forms — especially as folklore — the first of these papers being Alberto Cirese's "Concezioni del mondo, filo-

sofia spontanea, folclore" ("Conceptions of the World, Spontaneous Philosophy, Folklore").[10] The discussion of what today
would be called the sociology of literature, language, and culture
complemented the previous treatments of Gramsci's sociopolitical
aesthetics by highlighting the position that mass culture held in
Gramsci's political thought. Except for consideration of Gramsci's
reception abroad, this last set of papers, fittingly enough, brought
the two volumes of *Gramsci e la cultura contemporanea* to a close.

Examination of the other critical "event" of the mid-1960's mentioned above, the publication of Asor Rosa's critical study of *populismo* in modern Italian literature, leads to somewhat less enthusiastic, or at least less positive, conclusions. While denying neither
the potency of Gramsci's diligent historicism nor the vitality of his
interest in the sociology of literature, Asor Rosa condemns all
those writers, whether preceding or following Gramsci, who gave
any appearance of furnishing a potentially popular body of literature in Italy. For Asor Rosa, Italian literature is the expression of an
elite caste, not of *il popolo*, or "the people," and this is true be the
writer in question the nineteenth-century *romanesco*-dialect poet
Gioacchino Belli, with whom Asor Rosa's study begins, or Pier
Paolo Pasolini, with whom *Scrittori e popolo* ends. Truly "popular"
literature, in Asor Rosa's view, would need not only to express the
genuine perspective of the common people but also to offer the
populace as a social and ethical model to be *emulated* as well as
imitated. Neither Belli nor Pasolini nor anyone else in between
demonstrates such a combination, and this for a basic reason: modern Italian literature, in one way or another, represents not the
values of the "people" but rather the crisis of bourgeois ideology
and bourgeois society. In Asor Rosa's treatment, Italian literature,
from Vasco Pratolini's sketches of Florentine workingmen's quar-
ters to Pasolini's Roman narratives and poetry of incipient ideological commitment (such as *Le ceneri de Gramsci* [*The Ashes of Gramsci*] of 1957), thus suggests not so much that Gramsci was wrong to
have looked for examples of national-popular literature in modern
Italy as that the search itself was wrongheaded from the outset.

Asor Rosa's study, in spite of its negative tone and findings, did
indicate the fascination that Gramsci's critical and ethical catego-

ries continued to hold in postwar Italian aesthetics and in socio-political analysis. This Gramscian influence was also at work, in one way or another, in such political phenomena of the 1970's as the Communist Party's *compromesso storico,* or "historical compromise," and the various deliberations over the viability, scope, and goals of Eurocommunism; and both the letter and the spirit of Gramsci's works continued to show new life within various contemporary intellectual groups, in particular among the editorial group of *Il manifesto,* the radical journal of the Roman Left, and in the mid-1970's debate over Gramsci's ideas sponsored by the Socialist Party's monthly *Mondoperaio.*[11]

With a new era now under way — inaugurated, whether auspiciously or not, in the time of glasnost and perestroika with the installation of Achille Occhetto as secretary of the Italian Communist Party and continued with Massimo D'Alema's new leadership of the neo-Marxist Left — we are seeing a good deal of historical review and reevaluation of the major political figures of the Left during the 1920's and 1930's. As Occhetto announced in July 1988, shortly after his election, Togliatti is one of the primary objects of this process of study and reconsideration. Not only this actively reevaluative attitude but also the practical circumstance of the opening of the historical archives in Moscow should facilitate this work.[12] Nor is there any reason, within the realm of the Italian party, to stop with Togliatti. Indeed, a thoroughgoing historical review of Gramsci's writings and their influence, including the history of their use *and* abuse, would appear a timely task in Italy, to say the least. The question of the relations between culture and social change to which Gramsci's writings repeatedly returned are still, in the West, unresolved. Undoubtedly this lack of resolution helps explain the continuing fascination that Gramsci's work holds for writers imbued with both historical concerns and imaginative interests, writers such as Said, Jameson, and Aronowitz. The force and prophetic vision of Gramsci's thought make his lessons as instructive today as ever before.

8

Rationality and Myth in Pirandello's Later Works

Modernity, Contemporaneity, and the
Poetics of Historical Disillusionment

WHEN TAKEN TOGETHER, Luigi Pirandello's last novel, *Uno, nessuno e centomila* (1925–26; *One, None, and a Hundred Thousand*), and his last play, *I giganti della montagna* (*The Giants of the Mountain*, performed posthumously in 1937), combine to show the ends of two lines in Pirandello's thought.[1] The first of these lines, that of hyper-rational speculation based on the self-reflective structures of narcissism, culminates in the highly self-conscious and thoroughly ambiguous conclusion of *Uno, nessuno e centomila*. The second, that of equally speculative investigation into the historical yet irrational potentials of myth, comes to a close in *I giganti della montagna*. Although these two sets of concerns can be separated in theory for the purposes of analysis, in practice they are often interwoven through Pirandello's oeuvre. This is the case at least in part because the central issue on which both the rational and the irrational aspects of Pirandello's works focus is one and the same, the imaginative *and* historical relation between art and life. It would no doubt be heartening to be able to affirm that either one or the other of these lines of inquiry — or even each of them — eventually leads to a positive evaluation of the age-old art/life "problem." But despite the fact that Pirandello's late work does offer, through its various twists and turns, occasional glimpses of a positive historical resolution, neither a rational nor an irrational Pirandellian perspective in this regard ultimately gives rise to anything but the most pessimistic of views. It is true that the logical impasse that finally closes down the extreme rationality of Pirandello's narrative endeavors is countered in his last mythic dramas by an opening up to the seemingly visionary, future-oriented discourse of myth; but even then we are left with troubled and at best uncertain conclusions as to the relationship between art and life and, still more pointedly, as to the very viability of art as a genuine force in twentieth-century society.

These issues become considerably clearer not only when Pirandello is examined as a modernist writer but also when that critical examination itself is carried out from a more contemporary perspective, or more precisely, from a perspective that includes the discoveries of poststructuralist thought without being overpowered by the assumptions and practices of that thought. The results of this approach are threefold, and the advantages that they bring are interactive. First, Pirandello's art appears more firmly rooted in its own period, in the sociopolitical contests between liberalism and fascism and in the cultural crosscurrents of early twentieth-century Italy. Second, the elements of Pirandello's literary production that are still of interest today, after the surge of postmodern literature and poststructuralist critical analysis, stand out in sharper relief because many typically Pirandellian elements bear a distinct similarity to those of more recent works. And third, some of the bounds of poststructuralist thought show up more markedly, since the arc of Pirandello's last works carries us toward an incipient *critique* of the limitations of several recently influential poststructuralist varieties of the philosophy of reflection.

Because each of the two lines of thought on which we are focusing, the rational and the irrational, involves social as well as aesthetic and logical questions, they both entail not only analysis of literary and philosophical issues but also consideration of the basic characteristics of Italian social organization in the early part of the century. Pirandello's examination of social models that would offer alternatives to the traditional familial unit (and in particular to its petit bourgeois *fin de siècle* core) runs through a series of works from the opening years of the century on. In this respect, one need only consider the alternative versions of community evident in *Il fu Mattia Pascal* (1904; *The Late Mattia Pascal*), *Liolà* (1916), and *Enrico IV* (1922; *Henry IV*), alternatives that together eventually lead to the willfully "reasoned" destruction of any and all sense of community at the conclusion of *Uno, nessuno e centomila*. But the hyper-rationalistic aspect of Pirandello's works, his well-known "cerebration," does not really focus so much on society itself as on the individual, or, more accurately, on the individual thoroughly (and in the end irremediably) alienated from society. This is, to be sure, one of the standard concerns of modernist literature in its reaction against the often actively integrating forces of nineteenth-century narrative; and I have treated the modernist nature and effects of Pirandello's works in detail elsewhere.[2] But in this context a brief summary of Pirandellian alienation will eventually prove useful in coming to terms with the crucial differences between the rational and the irrational aspects of Pirandello's later works.

In *Uno, nessuno e centomila*, the main character, Vitangelo Moscarda ("Gengè," as his wife Dida affectionately refers to him), sets out to divest himself of all of the "constructions" of his life. Vitangelo's intent means, literally, the *scomposizione*, "decomposition," of the individual subject as a member of society. As the novel progresses, this highly rationalistic decomposition is carried out from two angles, one of them interpersonal and the other individual. Since Vitangelo is seen differently by everyone who views him (as banker, usurer, idler, incomprehensible oddball, and so forth), his being, for others *in toto*, is not only unstable but potentially infinite. Moreover, because Vitangelo — even for himself — is a new and different individual at each moment of progressive time, his own sense of himself *as* an individual is also shattered, now from within rather than merely from without. In Pirandellian terms, Vitangelo can see himself in his narcissian reflection in the mirror, but he cannot see himself live, because at the very moment of perception, life is already fleeting away. Ideally, Vitangelo could attempt to freeze time, to use his will to harden his identity for himself and for others into a fixed, unchanging, and unified truth, one that could then act as truth in the world. But in Pirandello's thought, such an ideal "truth" would succeed only by affirming the illusory stasis of form (*forma*) and thereby denying the vital, progressive reality of flux or, in Pirandello's terminology, that of life itself (*vita*). Pirandello's altogether alienated character is condemned not only to experience this impasse but also, in *Uno, nessuno e centomila*, to discover that there is no escape from it as long as he remains in society as society is currently constituted. It is this discovery that eventually leads to the novel's troubled and deeply ambiguous conclusion. In fact, the conclusion is so deeply ambiguous that, by the novel's end, the reader is left with the impossibility, at the basic level of narrative voice, of reconciling the speaking first-person subject *either* with the self-reflective objects of his discourse *or* with the product of his narration, which is to say, with the novel itself as a completed, unified aesthetic whole.

It is important to see that the roots of Pirandello's thought can be traced in earlier vitalist philosophies, such as those of Friedrich Nietzsche, Gabriel Séailles, and Henri Bergson, and that certain of Pirandello's interests parallel those of his futurist contemporaries. But it is equally important to consider Pirandello's vitalist concepts as they develop within his own work and especially within the growing aspects of his thought that have to do with the philosophy of reflection. This is a distinctively Pirandellian mix. The nodal concept of the dynamic opposition of life and form runs through Pirandello's early works, and it plays a significant role both in Pirandello's first mature novel, *Il fu Mattia Pascal*, and in the essay that Pirandello devoted to his special notion of self-reflective humor, entitled *L'umorismo* (1908; *On Humor*).[3] In the essay, Pirandello describes the characteristically contradictory and self-reflexive perspective of the *umorista*, who is constantly driven to decompose every apparently fixed or stable construction just as the active force of *vita* breaks down and diffuses every instance of stabilizing *forma*. In *Il fu Mattia Pascal*, these same categories are at work, but in terms of the *narrative* (as distinct from the self-reflective *narrator*), they show their effects in exactly the reverse order. That is, Mattia, having come to know of his own "death," sets out to construct the form of a new and workable character in the everyday world of society. But before too long, the resultant construction, the character Adriano Meis, is utterly undone by the multiple forces of life itself.

The fundamental problem in the earlier novel and in the essay as well — that art is obliged to construct (*comporre*) whereas the self-reflective life of the *umorista* is determined to decompose (*scomporre*) all such constructions — is reconsidered from differing angles in many of Pirandello's subsequent works, foremost among them *Enrico IV*, with its treatment both of painted images and of artfully crafted "history"; *Sei personaggi in cerca d'autore* (1921; *Six Characters in Search of an Author*), with its attempted re-creation in dramatic art of the family's truth in life; and *Uno, nessuno e centomila*, with its pointed discussion of the erotically inspired "misreading" of sculptured "reality" on the part of the unfortunately deluded Marco di Dio. All of these works involve Pirandellian considerations of the notion of the individual will, of the ability to take action for oneself and for others in a vital and meaningful way, and all of them provide implicit criticism of the very concept of authentic representation, that is, of the denial of difference in favor of identity in artistic, or indeed in *any*, re-creation. They all constitute, moreover, critiques of belief in the resultant created product, whether that product be seen in its predicament as a familial unit with a (perhaps) recountable familial history — as in *Così è (se vi pare)* (1917/1918; *It Is So [If You Think So]*) and in *Sei personaggi* — in its inherent epistemological contradictions as a *particular* instance of *conventional* language, or in its various failings as the affirmation of genuine, unified "characters" in the ordinary world of men and events.

Pirandello's view throughout these works, then, makes up a rational critique of the metaphorical organization of *form*, a critique that includes as its objects not only the inevitable metaphors of language itself but also the metaphors of the individual subject as a unified entity and of the family as a unit. The varieties of belief that permit such metaphorical representations to endure in human society are at every moment undercut, or, better, unmasked, by Pirandello's well-known skepticism, a skepticism that up to the late 1920's is so ingrained as to permit no alternative interpretation to stand on its own for very long. Before the mid-1920's Pirandello had stopped short of actually demonstrating where this self-reflexive process of individual and social dissolution might lead. But with the conclusion of *Uno, nessuno e centomila*, Pirandello takes the step that he had previously held back from, and he shows his character leaving organized society as well as any notion of the unified individual definitively behind. In an often-discussed section of the novel's concluding chapter, the narrator announces his break with established society, which means, for him, his break with the regulated metaphors for life that necessarily depend on the deceptions of form. Once again, though more succinctly than before in the novel, the narrator frames his announcement in terms of the functions of naming and the status of the individual subject:

Nessun nome. Nessun ricordo oggi del nome di jeri; del nome d'oggi, domani. Se il nome è la cosa; se un nome è in noi il concetto d'ogni cosa posta fuori di noi; e senza nome non si ha il concetto, e la cosa resta in noi come cieca, non distinta e non definita; ebbene, questo che portai tra gli uomini ciascuno lo incida, epigrafe funeraria, sulla fronte di quella immagine con cui gli apparvi, e la lasci in pace e non ne parli più. Non è altro che questo, epigrafe funeraria, un nome. Conviene ai morti. A chi ha concluso. Io sono vivo e non concludo. La vita non conclude. E non sa di nomi, la vita. Quest'albero, respiro trèmulo di foglie nuove. Sono quest'albero. Albero, nuvola; domani libro o vento: il libro che leggo, il vento che bevo. Tutto fuori, vagabondo.

No name. No memory today of yesterday's name; of today's name tomorrow. If the name is the thing, if a name in us is the concept of everything that is situated outside of us, and without a name there is no concept, and the thing remains blindly indistinct and undefined within us, very well, then, let everyone take that name which I once bore and engrave it as an epitaph on the brow of that image of me that they beheld; let them leave it there in peace and not speak of it again. For a name is no more than that, an epitaph. Something befitting the dead. One who has reached a conclusion. I am alive, and I reach no conclusion. Life knows no conclusion. Nor does it know anything of names. This tree, the tremulous breathing of new leaves. I am this tree. Tree, cloud; tomorrow, book or breeze: the book that I read, the breeze that I drink in. Living wholly without, a vagabond.[4]

In this crucial passage, names are rejected as externally fixed constructs, static, unchanging, and therefore illusory in their relation to what they supposedly name, which, in this context, is taken to be ever-shifting, vital, internal life. By establishing identity, names impose "objective" form on "subjective" life at the expense of life itself. Constructions, intellectual concepts, conclusions, even memory, as an imposition of static form on the vital fluidity of thought, are all to be eschewed in the narrator's new mode of being. The associations among form, stasis (along with abstractly conceptual or connected time), linguistic constructs, social organization, and death, all of which had been implicit in earlier sections of the novel, are here made pointedly clear. At the same time, the opposing elements of Pirandellian thought, vitality, flux (along with purely linear or constantly changing time), linguistic spontaneity, freedom, and life are valued as the primary characteristics of the narrator's new existence. Far from being the beginning of rational self-reflection, this new life represents, or perhaps it should be said, embodies, its end.

This resolution of the dialectics of *vita* and *forma* at the end of *Uno, nessuno e centomila*, a resolution that faces the crisis of *vita* and *forma* by abandoning the notion of fixed, reasoned form in favor of complete immersion in the vital stream of seemingly natural, nonrational and nonreflective life, does offer a solution of sorts to the novel's underlying problematic. But it is not the only solution possible, nor is it the only one to which Pirandello himself was drawn over the course of the following decade. As an alternative approach to the social problems implied, though not always specified, by the highly cerebral self-reflective line of thought culminating in *Uno, nessuno e centomila*, Pirandello turned with increasing interest to the irrational realm of myth. In general terms, this approach to social issues through mythic truth furnishes parallels with the works of such roughly contemporary authors as Yeats, Rilke, Lawrence, Lord Dunsany (whose mythic drama *The Gods of the Mountain* [1911] was performed by Pirandello's Teatro d'Arte di Roma in 1925), and Gabriele D'Annunzio (whose *Figlia di Iorio* [*Iorio's Daughter*] was given a special performance in 1934 under Pirandello's direction, with his stalwarts, Ruggero

Ruggeri and Marta Abba, as the leads). In Pirandello's mythic works, and particularly in the trilogy that he designated specifically as myths — *La nuova colonia* (1928; *The New Colony*), *Lazzaro* (1929; *Lazarus*), and *I giganti della montagna* — questions of social organization are addressed more directly than they had been in Pirandello's highly rational and oblique treatments, and they are also addressed more creatively than in his earlier naturalistic works depicting nineteenth-century Sicilian society, including *I vecchi e i giovani* (1909/1913; *The Old and the Young*). In dealing with these issues, Pirandello takes the same categories that he had considered on numerous previous occasions, those of perspective and belief, but at first he seems to shift their importance by giving the greatest emphasis to belief, and, indeed, to the primacy of faith itself.

This shift in emphasis is most forceful in the affirmation dramatized at the end of *Lazzaro*. What is it that is affirmed at the play's conclusion? The story of the drama has to do with the phenomenon of revivification, more precisely with the experience of the individual (here, Diego) during the period in which he is "dead." The problem posed at the drama's conclusion is directly concerned with the existence of God. If the character, once revivified, does not have any memory of God in the afterlife (as Diego does not), does this lack mean that there is no deity? Despite the skepticism of Diego and several of the other characters, the answer turns out to be that the recollection of the individual is immaterial, since God exists not outside of human beings but *within* them, in the *present* function of their faith. Memory of prior experience — be it natural or supernatural — is thus of no consequence. This concept of an immanent, individualized deity tied to the active belief of each and every human being recalls Vitangelo's abandonment, near the end of *Uno, nessuno e centomila*, of the stable "constructions" of organized religion in favor of the spontaneous and *genuine* interior sense of individual faith, what Vitangelo terms "il Dio di dentro," "the God within." *Lazzaro*, however, demonstrates a significant difference from the novel, because even though the workings of faith affirmed at the play's conclusion begin with *individually* experienced belief, they end with the presentation of a *communally* perceived and celebrated miracle, in Lia's sudden ability to rise from her wheelchair and walk. The play thus closes with an enactment of the powers of faith in a scene that metaphorically parallels Diego's (and, of course, Lazarus's) miraculous return to the world of the living.

Again, it is important to note that in *Lazzaro* the function of belief starts as a force within the individual and spreads outward to transform the behavior and the interrelations of human beings in a collective environment. In the process, Pirandellian skepticism is not utterly foregone but is instead subsumed in the overall category of belief, since intelligent faith *includes* the realization that one cannot know all (as the Monsignor, however overly doctrinaire, comments at one point, "Guaj a chi crede di sapere [tutto]!"; "Watch out if you believe you know [everything]!").[5] Faith — by definition belief in what one cannot rationally know — thus serves as a capstone to a much broader system of knowledge. This position, it should be noted, places considerably less emphasis not only on the previous Pirandellian dialectics of *vita* and *forma* but also on the individualized phenomenon of self-reflection so central to Pirandellian thought up to the end of *Uno, nessuno e centomila*.

Both the dramatic progression and the collective slant of *Lazzaro* run exactly contrary to the principles and the effects of many of Pirandello's earlier works, which characteristically end in individual expressions of doubt or consternation — or in the negative light of violence — rather than in communal affirmation. Although it is true that many systems of active belief are portrayed in earlier works, such systems are usually framed by overriding disbelief and/or by ironic questioning (such as — to take just a few of the numerous possible examples — the guarded presentation of Signor Paleari's theosophic preoccupations in *Il fu Mattia Pascal*, the clever manipulation of the motif of the immaculate conception in *Liolà*, the amalgam of skepticism and supernatural effects in *All'uscita* [1916/1922; *At the Exit*], and the expression of dismay with popular belief in traditional religion at the close of the *Sagra del Signore della Nave* [1924/1925; *Our Lord of the Ship*]). Works demonstrating rational skepticism do continue to show up in Pirandello's production after *Lazzaro*, but they do not demonstrate major advances on the line of reasoning already set forth in *Uno, nessuno e centomila*, nor are they really the appropriate companion pieces to be considered with *Lazzaro*, which are, rather, the two other parts of the mythic trilogy: the late drama of specifically artistic alienation, *Quando si è qualcuno* (1933; *When One Is Someone*); and the play that mixes popular and political "fable," *La favola del figlio cambiato* (1933/1934; *The Fable of the Changeling*).

This is an interesting if in many respects curious group of plays. In part because of the very success of Eric Bentley's extremely useful collection, *Naked Masks*, which does not include examples of the later mythic dramas, this crucial side of Pirandello's thought remains practically unknown in North America.[6] That myth was an extraordinarily important element in Pirandello's final literary production is evidenced not only by these dramas but also by the mythic novel on which he was at work when he died, tentatively entitled "Adamo ed Eva."[7] The first piece in the mythic trilogy, *La nuova colonia*, was described by Pirandello as a modern "mito sociale," or "social myth," while the others, *Lazzaro* and *I giganti*, were designated respectively as myths of religion and of art.[8] At issue in *La nuova colonia* is the possibility or impossibility of creating a society based on communal love and freedom. Although there are moments in the drama when belief in the effectiveness of social commitment for the common good seems to be affirmed, the drama's conclusion represents not this society's victory but rather its annihilation. In the following year comes *Lazzaro*, with, as we have seen, its striking affirmation of the individual and communal powers of belief. The conclusion of the third entry in the trilogy, *I giganti*, was thought out by Pirandello (and told to his son and colleague, Stefano) in the last night of his life. Before this final mythic drama, however, there intervened the two other plays in Pirandello's oeuvre that are especially germane in this context.

These dramas, *Quando si è qualcuno* and *La favola del figlio cambiato*, are important not just for their interest as artifacts, as artistic products, but also for what they tell us about Pirandello's developing relation to his art and to what he considered to be his social role as an artist. *Quando si è qualcuno* takes the prior dialectics of *vita* and *forma* and applies them to the situation of the successful artist living and working in society. As the artist be-comes visible and seemingly important apart from his work, which is to say, apart from the authentic, vital flow of artistic creation, he becomes an object on public display and thus suffers — to the detri-ment of *both* his art *and* his private sense of himself — the same fate that Vitangelo Moscarda had suffered as an individual in *Uno, nessuno e centomila*. The difference for the artist is, of course, that the writer, unlike Vitangelo, must remain living and working in society if his chosen task of artistic expression and communica-tion is to have any chance of success. The date of the opening of *Quando si è qualcuno* is of obvious import in relation to Piran-dello's growing stature as an internationally known playwright; indeed, the drama was first performed just one year before Piran-dello was awarded the Nobel Prize. The play demonstrates Piran-dello's increasing discomfiture with the role that his fame had cre-ated for him (a discomfiture that is far more bitter than such earlier expressions of displeasure as those found in *Sei personaggi*, *Cia-scuno a suo modo* [1924; *Each in His Own Way*], and *Questa sera si recita a soggetto* [1930; *Tonight We Improvise*]); yet, in its very function *as* theater, this play also attests, albeit secondarily, to Pi-randello's continuing commitment to the potential force of art as an ongoing social endeavor *despite* the trials that his renown brought with it.

Both of these concerns, the role of the artist (again with specific reference to Pirandello himself) and the place or function of art in society, lie at the heart of the relationship between *La favola del figlio cambiato* and *I giganti della montagna*. In terms of social belief, the lesson of *La favola del figlio cambiato* cuts in two di-rections at the same time. It affirms the validity and the vitality of popular, proverbially expressed wisdom (when coupled with deeply held individual commitment) while it calls into question — though perhaps "holds up to ridicule" would be more accurate — the self-sustaining and self-serving powers of political authori-tarianism. Needless to say, Pirandello's "fable" of the arbitrary and cruelly mendacious *forma* of political authority was less than pleasing to either its first European audience in Hitler's Germany (January 1934) or its first Italian audience in Mussolini's Rome

(March 1934). The condemnation of the *Favola* by both regimes was no doubt a blow to Pirandello, but equally galling, and in certain ways more so, was the public's reaction of complete incomprehension to his work. In spite of Pirandello's disappointment, however, he did not turn away from his mythic theater. He was so affected by this disaster that, rather than abandoning his attempts at mythic presentation, he used the story of *La favola del figlio cambiato* and its calamitous failure as the springboard for the events of *I giganti della montagna*. Pirandello thus persisted in his attempt to influence and inspire his audiences, to bring them around to his point of view, regardless of their highly vocal rejection.

I giganti opens with Cotrone (also called "il Mago," or "the Magician") among his group of "Scalognati" discussing the arrival of Ilse and her followers. As Ilse and the ragtag remnants of her theatrical company reach the magical villa, they begin to recite the play that they have been performing for two years in front of uncomprehending and thoroughly unappreciative audiences, *La favola del figlio cambiato*. The correspondences with Pirandello's work and with his existence as an artist are so close that the verses recited by Ilse and the others are in fact those of the previous drama; and even one major divergence from Pirandello's personal experience, the detail that the poet-author of *I giganti*'s "Favola" has committed suicide, establishes a subtle parallel, since the object of the deceased poet's affections, Ilse, has the role that in life was to be played by Pirandello's own beloved leading lady, Marta Abba.

I giganti's backdrop of artistic failure notwithstanding, the points regularly made through the first three "moments" (that is, through the two acts that Pirandello himself had written out prior to his death) deal not so much with art's failings as with its powers, as long as those powers are arrayed and set in motion in an appropriately conducive setting. This setting is, of course, the environment inside Cotrone's villa, where imaginative belief on the part of the company's individual actors is enough for them to realize their fantasies as reality, to make the objects of their imagination appear as real, palpable images in the world around them, in an *artistic* version, now with definite external effects, of Pirandello's earlier concept of "the God within." The mystically named villa "La Sca-logna" is, therefore, according to Cotrone, the perfect place for the performance of *La favola del figlio cambiato*, the one theatrical setting in which the drama literally cannot fail, any more than a dream can fail to be a genuine dream or than children's spontane-ously authentic beliefs can fail to make their imaginary games "true."

However tempting Cotrone's offer of the villa for recitation of the play might be, Ilse refuses for a single reason. As just about everyone on stage perceives, the entire drama and its truth remain alive inside Ilse (and indeed, when she begins to recite the dialogue to herself, in a remarkably "enchanting" voice, she recites all the parts, not merely her own). But for Ilse this is not sufficient. As she asserts at the end of the second act: "Vive in me; ma non basta! Deve vivere in mezzo agli uomini!" ("It lives within me; but that's not enough! It must live among mankind!").[9] Staying inside Co-trone's wondrous villa, where the powers of belief and imagination permit him and others to create new realities, or, as is repeated at several points, "inventare la verità," "to invent the truth," is simply not adequate to fulfill what Ilse regards as her artistic "mission."[10]

Ilse's continuing insistence, along with Cotrone's aid and the others' acquiescence, sets the stage for the drama's disconcerting and remarkably violent conclusion. Whether or not Stefano Piran-dello's version of this scene is completely acceptable, one part of the play's conclusion is beyond doubt: there is simply no place for genuine art in modern society as that society (including both its cultural and its political makeup) stands at the present moment. Pirandello's inclusion of the "olivo saraceno," the ancient olive tree with its symbolic redolence of ageless popular imagery and cultural wisdom, suggests that the forces of art, of the creative imagination expressing itself in and through artistic products, are not forever defeated, even by the economically fetishistic, obsessively authori-tarian, and culturally ignorant (or better, indifferent) society of the times, which is to say the current socioeconomic mixture of rising bourgeois capitalism and state-sponsored fascism. But it is thor-oughly obvious, given the extended violence of the scene, that true art, for the moment, is in both symbolic and real terms dead.

To just what degree artists—as "fanatics" of art equally oblivious to real life as the "fanatics" of life are to art—must share the guilt for this state of affairs remains in question at *I giganti*'s close irrespective of Stefano Pirandello's assertions, as Marta Abba has pointed out in her highly critical discussion of Stefano's version.[11] But, to repeat, the implications that the drama's fourth and final moment has for the fate of artists and their art in contemporary Italian society are if anything all too clear. In this society, art can exist comfortably only *apart from* society, not within it. Artists really are "scalognati," or the symbolic victim/heroes of the "evil eye," and their most imaginative works, like even the most marvelous furnishings of Cotrone's villa, really are regarded only as "superfluous."[12] As distinct from the conclusion of the previous entry in the trilogy, at the end of *I giganti* there are no miracles to revivify the public's belief in art, only the rejected Magician and the weary troupe of players carrying off Ilse's broken, puppetlike corpse.

This ending, it should be apparent, is far more pessimistic than similar passages in the earlier trilogy of "the theater in the theater" or even in *Quando si è qualcuno* (i.e., public incomprehension and rejection turned out, for Pirandello, to be finally worse than public incomprehension and celebration). Although in the late 1920's, myth's compelling wholeness had provided Pirandello with a way around some of the paralyzing effects of his compulsively fragmented and cerebrally self-reflexive works, it no longer seemed to function, as far as art was concerned, after Pirandello's social and theatrical experiences of the early and mid 1930's. His last play, doomed to stay "al limite, fra la favola e la realtà" ("at the limit between fable and reality"),[13] could not lead either its author or its characters back into society. True, it is the drama's *character* Ilse who dies at the play's conclusion, but at this juncture we might do well to remember that her poet/author, the author of *La favola del figlio cambiato*, had at least in symbolic terms committed the socially self-exclusionary gesture of suicide even before the action of *I giganti* had begun. There is no room, in this world, for the two absolute requirements of Pirandello's developing aesthetic: unrelenting belief in the power of art and unrelenting belief in the *po-*

tential of human society. In Pirandello's view, only the inventive forces of art working in society would give rise to a new and better world, but this was also the one combination of art and life that Pirandello felt, at his death, to be hopelessly unviable. At the close of *I giganti*, the adepts of neither side, neither of art nor of life, could see to what extent and in what ways each needed the other.

Reconsideration of Pirandello's oeuvre in its entirety shows that the energy behind his works—which is also the primary social characteristic of modernist literature—springs from the crisis of the individual in relation to the contemporary environment of bourgeois society from which the subject appears ever more alienated. Again typical of most modernist authors, Pirandello demonstrates his concerns in direct relation to the society of his times, even if the political, economic, and familial traits and values of that society are portrayed, at the depths of his works, only as elements to be reacted against. Throughout Pirandello's highly rationalistic works, he focuses on the category so dear to modernism, not that of individual desire alone but that of the individual will, which is to say, the mixture of aspiration, action, and frustration, in short, individual conflict—the category that informs so much of the literature of his historical moment. But Pirandello also saw, by the late 1920's, that merely staying at the level of the individual subject to elucidate the underlying opposition of *vita* and *forma* (at its extreme, the opposition of life and death) and then, in poststructuralist manner, to decompose, unmask, or, to use another term, deconstruct this opposition's products was insufficient to arrive at the category with which in the end he was most involved, that of human society itself.

This final concern led Pirandello beyond the rational critique of the "falsity" of the individual subject to the affirmation of the collective "truth" of myth. This move, as we have seen, was ultimately unsuccessful. Going beyond the reasoned, self-reflective analysis of the inevitable *méconnaissance* at the center of the metaphors by which man lives, metaphors of the individual, of language, of art, and of society, in order to arrive at the artistic assertion of the importance of collective belief and of the viability of collective action did not bring Pirandello to a positive or lasting view of social life. Nevertheless, the basic urge not only to work through but also to continue *beyond* such typically poststructuralist, or again, deconstructive, interests lends Pirandello's work a specifically *post*-postmodern cast. That is to say, Pirandello's later attention to the imaginative possibilities of community, of artistic creation as a social force, and of genuine collective authority provides what we may consider *both* an acknowledgment of the limits of his own earlier works *and* an incipient criticism of the eventual varieties of the philosophy of reflection that remain at the level of the individual subject (such as Lacanian psychoanalysis), at that of language (such as Derridean deconstruction), at that of strictly idealized "history" (such as many, though not all, Foucauldian archeologies of knowledge), or at that of programmatically ahistorical and nonauthoritarian thought (such as Vattimo's *pensiero debole*). In brief, there is no analytic truth that can claim social validity without consideration of the material facts of social history and social authority, and it was Pirandello's experience as an author and a man, caught in the crisis of everyday life for the socially oriented artist between the two wars, that brought him, even though reluctantly, to this conclusion.

It is also true, of course, that this conclusion, in and of itself, did not yield further felicitous results. This is the case for a particular reason, one that is made clear at the conclusion of *I giganti della montagna*, Pirandello's bleak *Tempest*. To state it directly, Pirandello's public did not want — or worse, was unable — either to appreciate or to understand what he was trying to do with his art. The audience's reaction in Pirandello's historical *present* made it impossible for his criticisms and his suggestions for the *future* to gain a purchase. Pirandello's last gambit, the move away from analytic skepticism toward mythic affirmation, demonstrated an obvious point of vulnerability, moreover, because his sense of myth, though it included Cotrone's traditional concept of what the "ancients" knew and what the populace "has *always* known,"[14] was not really geared toward a Vichian examination of the supposedly "mythic" evidence of the past, not toward consideration solely of roots or origins, but rather toward the imaginative future, toward visionary prophecy. That in Pirandello's time his aspirations as an artist went unheeded by certain of his closest supporters as well as by his many detractors (including earlier fascist *carissimi*) tells us at least as much about Pirandello's public under the fascist regime as it does about Pirandello himself.[15] At Pirandello's death, the movement past individual and social dissolution to imaginative reconstitution, based on the vital workings of belief and on the intervention of wondrous *invention* in the cultural reality of social life, remained for the artist, however heartfelt, only an aspiration. This is another way of saying that unlike Cotrone's ardent follower, La Sgricia, in the marvelous insert-story in *I giganti della montagna*, Pirandello would find in the growing darkness of the mid-1930's no beneficent Angelo Centuno with troops from the world beyond to save either the artist or his art.

9

Literary Representation and Sociopolitical/ Cultural Contexts in the Historical Novel

Morante, Faulkner, Vargas Llosa

Two of the major narrative concerns of Elsa Morante's *La Storia* (1974; *History*) are the essence and uses of imaginative poetry (or, broadly considered, creative fantasy), of which she provides a forceful critique, and the very possibility or impossibility of poetry's continued existence in the historical world of everyday life.[1] These concerns, when viewed in the context of the novel's amalgam of Christian and Marxist ethical polemics, mark *La Storia* as a literary product of an important though concisely delimited era in Italian cultural life, roughly that following the social and political quake of 1968 and preceding the peculiar series of aftershocks during the years 1976–80. The ties that link Morante's novel to its own time are even stronger than those of her subsequent novel, *Aracoeli* (1982), or of her two previous novels, *Menzogna e sortilegio* (1948; *House of Liars*) and *L'isola di Arturo* (1957; *Arthur's Island*). In *La Storia*, what the accumulated meaning of these concerns points up is, first, the social trial of poetry in the modern world and, second, the tremendous stake that all mankind has in that trial's outcome.

This self-conscious ordeal, though not its conclusion, is what

Morante's narrative in its totality eventually comes to represent in a fashion that I will contrast to equally compelling but very different historical novels by William Faulkner and Mario Vargas Llosa. However, since *La Storia* is a historical novel, with a consequent commitment to worldly representation, Morante's self-reflexive portrayal of the ordeals that poetry must endure is presented first of all as a part of ordinary, day-to-day existence, solidly rooted in the life and times of the narrative's main historical period, the years during and immediately following World War II. At the same time, though in indirect ways, the novel's *own* poetic aspects are also presented as participating in this everyday process. In part because of the narrative's realistically framed *poetic* self-reflexivity, *La Storia*'s poetic and representational procedures combine to form an aesthetically unified yet extremely disturbing picture of the novel's principal subject matter, the lives of a simple, half-Jewish schoolteacher, Ida Ramundo, her children, and their familial acquaintances in war-torn Rome. The complexity of Morante's narrative derives from the multiplicity of this representational *and* poetic focus, since on one level the novel portrays the family's everyday experiences, while on another it depicts the difficulties of the worldly functioning of creative fantasy, and on a third it inserts its own discourse into that same set of difficulties, in a mixture of *overtly* historical and *covertly* contemporary social representation and diagnosis. In view of the text's bulk of more than six hundred pages, Morante's ability to keep this juggling act going over the course of the entire novel without giving up either her commitment to representation or her interest in poetry's worldly fate attests to the depth as well as to the breadth of her outlook.

The variety of these narrative concerns — for the representation of historical events through the experiences of a restricted group of characters and for the functions of the creative imagination within those experiences — is signaled even prior to the story's beginning, on the book's title page, which reads in full: *La Storia, Romanzo*, or *History: A Novel*. The side of this apparent dialectic that is most often treated by the novel's critics, although with several notable exceptions, is that of "History." History itself, in Morante's conception, subdivides into History with a capital "H," that is, the official History of economic power and international politics, and history with a small "h," the daily lives of the little people who make up the vast, unsung preponderance of the world's population. Within the novel, the machinations of History are discussed and, most often, denigrated by the openly self-identifying narrator in the broadly evaluative historical sections inserted into *La Storia*'s primary discourse, which, again, is constituted by the highly detailed representation of the daily lives of Ida and her offspring.

Although *La Storia* is cast in the mold of a historical novel, any attempt to read it merely as an example of seemingly transparent, representational fiction will be frustrated both by these purposefully slanted Historical introductions and by the spontaneously self-conscious and often pointedly challenging interruptions of the narrator. It is not hard to see, as one progresses through the novel, that this is realism in the line of Brecht rather than of Auerbach or even Lukács. It is true that, in terms of the aesthetics of literary models and effects, this sort of realism — in which the reader is repeatedly reminded *both* of his or her position as reader *and* of the responsibility for interpretation entailed by any representation of "History" *or* "history" — does disrupt the conventions of traditional realist discourse. But this result takes on even greater importance in *La Storia* when the book's first audience is considered from a historical perspective, and more narrowly, from that of Italian political history.

The year 1974 was by no means insignificant in Italian culture, but by any measure it was part of an inestimably momentous period for Italian politics. Under Enrico Berlinguer, the recently elected secretary of the Communist Party, it appeared to many, including writers, academics, journalists, and others associated with the Italian Left, that new solutions to Italy's age-old social and political problems might actually be on the horizon. Questions like the status of the family, the social role of women, the possible reorganization of the Italian economy (following the end of the postwar "economic miracle" and the 1973–74 crisis), and the reform of countless other institutions from the universities to the labor unions to the press were being regularly addressed throughout the country. In this highly politicized and often heady environment, it is not surprising that Morante's patently political novel created a stir. I have discussed elsewhere the publishing aspects of *La Storia*'s initial success (in terms of marketing and publicity "hype") and the literary elements of its critical reception (in terms of the breakup and decline of the previous avant-garde of the "Gruppo 63" and other neo-experimentalists).[2] In this context, it may suffice to remark that upon *La Storia*'s appearance in 1974, the Italian Left, riding on the surge of optimism of the early 1970's — prior to the massive setback, and ensuing confusion, at the polls in 1976 — found itself less than comfortable with a book as pessimistic and as depressing, and in particular as insistently prodding, as Morante's novel.

Even though the pertinence and the force of the novel's statement and the historical climate of its reception can easily be lost on subsequent generations (and different nationalities) of readers, the circumstances of the book's initial appearance should not be taken lightly. By confronting head-on such topics as sociopolitical oppression and victimization; potentially non-Freudian, spontaneous love; and the relation between utopian anarchism, Marxism, and millenarian Christianity (ranging from Davide Segre's theory of infinitely multiple Christs, all recognized by their use of the same word, to little Useppe's angelic and "poetic" goodness), Morante's novel staked out positions in several of the most besieged regions of the social, political, and cultural debates in the early and mid-1970's. That the book was a work of fiction, and therefore one that required from its readers reflection and interpretation before its place in those debates could be assessed, only made the public's reaction to it that much more complicated. This was true in emotional as well as intellectual terms, all the more so owing to the strange mixture of representational responsibility, ironic withdrawal, and pathos that both infuses and derives from the narrator's voice.

Nowhere is this distinctive mixture more apparent than at the novel's conclusion, in the scene of Ida's reaction to Useppe's death.[3]

The scene begins with Useppe's lifeless body on the floor of the apartment's entryway where he fell; his feet are bare, since his little sandals had fallen off, and his arms are spread out in the attitude of Christian sacrifice. When Ida returns to the apartment, her reaction to what has happened is to imagine that all the terrors in the history of the world have come together to produce this end:

Ora nella mente stolida e malcresciuta di quella donnetta, mentre correva a precipizio per il suo piccolo alloggio, ruotarono anche le scene della storia umana (la Storia) che essa percepí come le spire multiple di un assassinio interminabile. E oggi l'ultimo assassinato era il suo bastarduccio Useppe. Tutta la Storia e le nazioni della terra s'erano concordate a questo fine: la strage del bambinello Useppe Ramundo.

Now in the stolid and undeveloped mind of that little woman, as she ran wildly around her small home, the scenes of human history (History) also revolved, which she perceived as the multiple coils of an interminable series of murders. And today the last to be murdered was her little bastard son, Useppe. All History and the nations of the earth had agreed on this end: the slaughter of the little child Useppe Ramundo.

As had occurred earlier in the course of Davide's drunken discourse, the narrator again concurs in Ida's bitter accusation against human history and refines that condemnation by casting history in the narrator's own terminology as History. At this point it appears, therefore, that regardless of Ida's severe limitations she has at last understood her plight in the very terms in which the narrator conceives of the world's situation. The next step in the development of this scene, moreover, seems to extend the nature of Ida's understanding. The smile that she has been futilely waiting to see on Useppe's face appears instead, by a "miracle," on her own face. Ida's reaction links her even more closely to Useppe's experience since, as the narrator notes, her smile is similar to the expression of marvelous innocence and quietude that earlier had accompanied her own seizures.[4] But the suggestions that Ida has now understood Useppe's fate as well as her own circumstances both in an intellectual sense and in an emotional, even miraculously spiritual one are immediately undercut by the narrator herself, who in an uncannily disconcerting conclusion, once again tinged with pathos *and* irony, explains that Ida's response was neither the smile of rational understanding nor that of revelation but instead that of madness. With this, Ida's life, as the narrator goes on to note, effectively ends, and "la povera storia di Iduzza Ramundo era finita" ("the poor history of Iduzza Ramundo was finished").

This conclusion, or something very much like it, was most likely inevitable from the start, given the narrative's view of History. Like many earlier twentieth-century writers, though in a more deeply political manner, Morante sees that all History is nothing but a story of sickness, oppression, and death: in the end, no one escapes alive. Morante's History thus evinces its force in the world of history just as pervasively and as powerfully as Vico's or Manzoni's Providence, but its effects, by contrast, are always negative. Significantly enough, Morante sees not only the problems of the historical world of matter and sense but also a solution to those problems, at least *in potentia*. That solution, quite simply, is the end of History itself. Unfortunately, *La Storia*, as a historical novel, can *suggest* such a solution but cannot *represent* it, since the desired end is not yet part of the everyday world.

Two of the major ways in which the narrative makes this suggestion have been mentioned before: first, through the figure of Useppe and, second, through the agency charged with the task of representation, the narrative voice. Whereas Useppe is the walking embodiment of poetry and of innocent love as well as the novel's principal indication of human potential in a non-oedipal, evangelical future, the increasing pessimism of the narrative voice regularly serves to remind the reader that, as long as History holds sway, the utopian potential of mankind can never be realized.

Morante's book thus takes its place in the highly charged political atmosphere of the Italian mid-1970's not only as a literary depiction of social life but also as a social statement and a political accusation. The political purposes of art had been part of Morante's developing aesthetics for some time, but with the publication of *La Storia* they entered their most intense stage. In a series of remarks to a union-sponsored cultural conference in Rome in 1976, following the censoring of the text of *La Storia* in Franco's Spain, Morante explained the goals of her book in no uncertain terms.[5] Provided with this opportunity, she used it to reaffirm the dual nature of *La Storia* as both a "work of poetry" and "an act of accusation against all the fascisms of the world." Her book thus represents, for her, what Useppe had represented *within* her narrative, a worldly example of the force of poetry, of creative imagination at work in the world, and a key to the understanding and the salvation of human society gone wrong, which is to say, to the understanding of history *and* History. On this topic at the same conference, Morante was at once eloquent and concise: "[*La Storia* is] an urgent and desperate request, which is directed at *everyone*, to the end of a possible *communal awakening*."

This affirmation picks up the self-consciously expressed concern in the narrative for the worldly power of poetry, while it casts that concern in a decidedly political light. To conceive of Morante's aesthetics for a moment in terms of Benjamin's concept of the "aura," the traditional aura of the work of art has returned in the form of the political richness of representational fiction's authentic worldly *force*. Morante's book thus becomes a self-conscious work of art with a new twist, since the circle of that self-consciousness — of poetry as a factor within the narrative and of the novel itself as a poetic factor in the world of its reception — is completed only as the novel enters the empirical world of its audience. By putting in question the future of human society through depiction of the recent historical past, and, in the fashion of a Brechtian epos, by then placing the burden of responsibility for understanding and *change* on the novel's readers, *La Storia* strains at the limits of the form of the historical novel, indeed at the limits of literary representation itself. *La Storia* may thus be seen as an attempt at creating a special sort of *romanzo popolare* (to borrow a notion from Gramsci), one that, despite the critical misunderstanding that greeted the novel's publication, intends not only to represent the day-to-day world of popular society but also to take its place in that world as a thorn in the side of its audience.

This type of literary *and* political self-consciousness was new in Italian postwar fiction. Given this novelty, the difficulties in classifying the narrative — and indeed of reacting to it in any coherent fashion — that were so apparent in the course of the debate following its appearance are perhaps understandable. There had been, of course, many previous Italian narratives with obvious political subject matter and ideological evaluation — the examples of D'Annunzio and Ignazio Silone come immediately to mind — but never before had literary self-consciousness itself cut so close to the heart of what it meant to be at one and the same time a work of art *and* a statement of political belief. None of this means that the intent of Morante as an individual author was sufficient to produce the results for which she hoped, any more than the wills of her most "poetic" characters — Davide and especially Useppe — are enough to change their own world. Both at the end of her novel and at the end of her conference remarks in 1976, Morante noted, with obvious despair, "And History continues" — as did in her view, therefore, the daily trial of poetry itself.

At this point, I would like to move on to a consideration of William Faulkner's *Absalom, Absalom!* (1936) and of Mario Vargas Llosa's *La guerra del fin del mundo* (1981; *The War of the End of the World*), by emphasizing, however briefly, a set of interests, some of which up to now have been implicit rather than explicit. First and foremost among these is our principal and explicit point of reference, that is, the relation between the sociopolitical period described within the historical novel and that of the novel's own creation and initial publication. Second is the degree of distance in the perspective from which the novel's story is told, that is, whether the narrative is related from "inside" or "outside" the psychological frame of its protagonists and events. Third — and this point is, of course, closely tied to the former — is the tense of narrative description, whether present or past, seemingly immediate or seemingly distanced (which is again a question of degree). And, fourth, though this last concern must of necessity remain murky until the others have been taken up, is the nature of the *overall* view of human history that the novels under consideration, by means of the sleight of hand of novelistic discourse, at once grow out of, embody, and propagate.

The basic parallels between the events of Canudos as portrayed in Vargas Llosa's *La guerra del fin del mundo* and more recent sociopolitical phenomena in rural Brazil (and especially in the Amazon basin) are fairly well known even outside of Latin America, as is evidenced, to give just one example, by the account in a Milan daily, the influential *Corriere della sera* (Nov. 1, 1985), of the fate of a band of mercenary *fazenderos* caught in the midst of a peasants' revolt. This revolt eventually drew the reaction of the Brazilian Army, in the region that the Italian correspondent termed with obvious delight the "Far West" of Brazil. (The story was published in the same week that the *Corriere* ran an interview with Vargas Llosa himself.) To proceed with our points of concern, Vargas Llosa's novel, like Morante's *La Storia*, is narrated in the third person. The narrative thus gives the impression of remaining predominantly outside its characters' perspectives, though *La guerra del fin del mundo*, in contrast to *La Storia*, has no single self-identifying or even stable narrative voice. The most prevalent narrative tense used in *La guerra del fin del mundo*, the present, contributes to the effects of narrative simultaneity for which Vargas Llosa is justly renowned and again differentiates his novelistic technique from that of the carefully controlled past tense used in *La Storia*. However, where investigation of these differences in technique eventually *leads*, which is to say, beyond questions of narrative technique and into questions of narrative meaning, will become considerably clearer if we take a moment to consider Faulkner's *Absalom, Absalom!* in the light of these same historical and literary concerns.

Faulkner's novel, as is well known, represented a break with the assumptions and procedures of the historical novel up to its time in Europe and in America. Although it is true that Faulkner's humanist portrayal of a young man's *pre*–World War I attempt to come to terms with the heritage of the "Old South" had definite and important parallels in the sociopolitical *post*–World War I era of its reception (in the tribulations of the new "New South"), and thus demonstrated the same sort of historical byplay we have been considering as part of the historical novel in general, both *Absalom, Absalom!*'s literary techniques and its effects on its audience were quite different from those of traditional historical novels. One of the reasons for this difference was that Faulkner narrated the events of the story from inside his characters' perspectives (from the historical first person, usually in extended dialogue). This technique differs from those of Morante and Vargas Llosa. Faulkner's manipulation of the temporal aspects of the narration, however, puts him somewhere between the other two writers. Whereas the general tense of narration in *Absalom, Absalom!* is the historical past (somewhat as in *La Storia*) the Quentin-Shreve frame story is given as the present of the narration *in toto* (somewhat as in *La guerra del fin del mundo*), with the result that present and past, fluid simultaneity and ordered discrimination, impinge on each other and thus constantly require the reader to struggle to define and redefine the basic temporal relations of the narrative as a whole.

Whereas these differences in narrative technique are important, none of them is as significant as the underlying difference that such techniques, taken together, begin to suggest. This has to do not only with the details of tense or perspective but also, and far more pressingly, with the differing views of human history itself that these novels both reflect and evince. To continue with Faulkner's work (which, true, was read and admired in Europe — the reactions of Sartre and Vittorini come immediately to mind — but which functioned moreover as a working model for an entire generation of Latin American writers, including Vargas Llosa), it is fairly easy to see that the view of human history exhibited by *Absalom, Absalom!* is not a rational or reasoned "scientific" one (as in, *grosso modo*, *La Storia*) but instead a thoroughly relativistic, irrational "anthropological" one (as in *La guerra del fin del mundo*). The effects of this anthropological perspective can be seen in many of the narrative's details, for example, the wild Negro driver racing out of the wilderness into church (at Sutpen's instigation and to the consternation of the townspeople), the sight of Judith in the loft watching in fascination as her father fights bare-chested with one of his own Negroes, or the eventual haggling over the relative merits and demerits of miscegenation and incest. But the perspective itself is also clear in Faulkner's *entire* conception of the vast panoply of the history of the South, from the realm of the Indians, to the first white settlers, to the aristocracy of the old South and the tragedy of the Civil War, to the question of the people of the new South, who, however, like Quentin, cannot quite escape the burden of their past despite all their attempts at exorcism (to which, of course, we owe the novel itself).

This shift in the historical novel away from the perspective of "rational science" toward that of totalizing anthropology, toward a *new* scientific discourse whose object is not nature or even man as a rational being but instead language and myth, reflects a parallel contextual shift from the Darwinian model of natural science toward the model of anthropology as nineteenth-century thought and culture develop into our own era. Along with differences over time, these two versions of investigative totality also demonstrate differences in national — or here, continental — cultural orientation, since, as both Roberto González Echevarría and Sara Castro-Klarén have noted, the new perspective of the anthropological novel is especially characteristic of contemporary Latin American narrative (and I mean to add Faulkner's *Absalom, Absalom!* here as a model) whereas the historical novel in Europe remains by and large tied to its own lengthy tradition of "scientific" investigation.[6]

None of this, of course, means jettisoning Darwin and Marx; as regards narrative vision, it means only adding to them Jung, Oswald Spengler, and, still closer to our own time, Lévi-Strauss. Although the differences between Morante and Vargas Llosa in this regard are fairly clear (despite their apparent similarity in narrative from the "outside"), they attain a far more definite focus when the mediating model of Faulkner is taken into account. True, the play between historical and *contemporary* sociopolitical contexts in all three of these novels remains in force, but now in the light of two differing views as to what human history is and as to how its truth is to be perceived and re-presented. If all this seems more a return to the model of Greek tragedy than a step into the American and Latin American cultural future, one need only recall another salient anthropological example of the modern novel, that great European *pre-postmodern* work drenched in the lore of language and myth as well as in that of cultural history, *Finnegans Wake*. This final reference should be enough to suggest the imaginative blurring of what have up to now, in my own presentation, seemed all-too-neat distinctions between European and American (including Latin American) literary traditions. These distinctions, indeed, are graded, not rigid. In any case, to return to the subject with which we began, it is important to acknowledge *in fine* that Morante's novel itself contains the seed — though only that — of the *anthropological* concerns of Faulkner and Vargas Llosa, in *La Storia*'s own imaginative presentation of the first, and perhaps the last, innocent poet of the modern age, the Vichian poet-hero who in the end falls silent beneath the march of History, the wondrous child Useppe.

PART THREE

THREE DEBATES

10

"The Exercise of Silence"

Reflections on the Controversy
over Paul de Man

Roughly a decade ago, while engaged in archival work in preparation for a doctoral thesis on Paul de Man, a Belgian research student named Ortwin de Graef made a disconcerting discovery: in the early 1940's de Man had written a series of articles, several with a notably anti-Semitic cast, for Belgian newspapers then under Nazi control. By the summer of 1987, when word of de Graef's discovery began to reach colleagues in the United States and elsewhere, the number of articles in question already appeared considerable, well over one hundred. In the following months, estimates of the size of de Man's wartime output continued to increase, until the number of articles seemed to be approximately three hundred. As more material turned up, the period of de Man's journalistic writing also expanded past the initially hypothesized terminal date of 1942 into 1943. This ending date is of some significance because it carries the period of de Man's writing well beyond the start of full-fledged Nazi oversight of journalistic and literary output and also beyond the terminal date furnished by de Man himself in the draft of an explanatory letter, since much quoted, dated September 1954, addressed to the director of the Harvard Society of Fellows, in which de Man gave a brief account of his journalistic activities during the occupation.

It is not strange that a man in his early twenties with a young family to support would turn to the pursuit he knew best, literary criticism, in order to make a living. Nor is it strange — extremely unfortunate, but not strange, given the horrible situation in Belgium and the rest of Europe — that anyone writing publicly in an occupied country would adopt, at least to an extent, the general perspectives and biases of the occupying forces. And de Man did intend to write and to continue writing publicly: that is confirmed by his prodigious productivity. He was publishing in *Le Soir*, an important, established Belgian newspaper, one that provided him with a forum worthy of the brilliant nephew of Hendrik de Man, Belgium's best-known political thinker (indeed, well enough known in the 1920's and 1930's that Gramsci, in his prison notebooks, mentions Hendrik de Man in the same contexts in which he mentions Croce, Lenin, Sorel, Eduard Bernstein, Rosa Luxemburg, et al., though Gramsci also expresses anything but admiration for the elder de Man's success, at one point deriding his work as "mediocrissimo").[1] True, the recent revelations concerning the World War II beliefs and activities of figures like Martin Heidegger, Maurice Blanchot, Hans Robert Jauss, and others contributed to the highly sensitized climate in which the disclosure of de Man's 1940's journalism was made. But the mere *fact* of de Man's writing during this period would have not been enough to explain either the extraordinary upheaval in intellectual circles caused by that disclosure or the extraordinary regimen of silence to which de Man himself adhered for over forty years, a regimen so strict that, at his death in 1983, few if any of his colleagues in the United States knew more than the vaguest outlines of his life and work during the war, and virtually no one knew the true nature and extent of his writing over that period.

This, then, is Paul de Man's silence, the "hive of secrets" eloquently described by Jacques Derrida in a tormented article in *Critical Inquiry*.[2] This silence was broken first, however discreetly, by de Graef and then, with shocking abruptness for the vast preponderance of de Man's friends and colleagues, by an article in the

New York Times on December 1, 1987 ("Yale Scholar's Articles Found in Nazi Paper"), an article that, for all its inaccuracies and blatant misrepresentations, was neither better nor worse than the many clumsy attempts subsequently made to publicize the de Man "scandal" in the American press (including articles in *Newsweek*, *Time*, *The Nation*, the *New York Times Magazine*, and numerous other newspapers and journals). There is certainly a good deal more that needs to be said about having such an intricate matter introduced to the American public by way of journalistic presentation.[3] Both the degree of inaccuracy of the newspapers' portrayal of de Man's behavior and the character of de Man's articles themselves doubtless are now clearer, since these articles, along with commentaries on them, have been published in two volumes, *Wartime Journalism 1939–1943* and *Responses*.[4] But still more noteworthy here than the representation of de Man's activities in the national and international press and the concomitant reaction, or absence of it, on the part of the public at large is the reaction of those literary critics close to de Man in the American and European academic arena, and most pointedly those who regard themselves as friendly to de Man's memory and his work. Indeed, it has not been the behavior of de Man's opponents but of his confreres and followers — and, suddenly, defenders — that has revealed most about the uncanny effects that de Man's presence had on the American academic environment. Before considering a few of those effects, however, a brief account of de Man's early writings themselves is in order.

The articles overall demonstrate a fairly consistent set of characteristics. The most notable of these is the intellectual ambition of their author. Even as a young man, whether discussing the works of single writers — from Joyce and Virginia Woolf to Goethe, Paul Valéry, and Jacques Chardonne — or such general trends as the sociocultural disorder between the two wars or the inward psychological turn of the modern novel, de Man wrote with a breadth of reference and an authority that can only be termed striking. This is not to say that de Man's critical voice in this period is either mature or wholly convincing. The errors of critical assessment and, on occasion, of critical omission as well as the quirks of judgment — so apparent when the subject is English literature but also at work here and there throughout these pieces — give continual evidence of de Man's youth. Indeed, the very bravado of his choice of topics and his critical presentation attests both to the youthful nature of his self-assurance, abetted by the traditional critical blindness of journalistic hubris, and, it may be, to the youthful desire to measure up to the expectations that accrued to him from the authority of his uncle and mentor, a figure who was perhaps not only literally but also figuratively, as has been suggested from time to time, his true "Dutch uncle."[5]

The ambition infusing de Man's intellectual vantage point also extends to his construction of national schemas. It is certainly the case that allusion to national character, national strengths and weaknesses, and national destinies was part and parcel of the rhetoric of the time. But in de Man's articles the belief in such notions, often elaborated quite vigorously and at some length, appears entirely genuine. Geoffrey Hartman describes de Man's position in this way: "A cultural nationalist, de Man believed in the 'genius' or the 'individual soul' of a people, in their 'unanimity' as it was attested by a shared language, a homeland, and an ancestral achievement."[6] Though Hartman goes on to characterize de Man's stand as a "common sort of nationalism," the position is asserted so forthrightly in de Man's articles and in such a wide variety of contexts that the proper term would seem to be not "nationalism" but cultural racism, with the strongest national contrast lying between what were, for the Belgian de Man, the two major forces in European thought and letters, the French on the one hand and the Germans on the other. In de Man's view, the attributes typical of the French "genius" are cerebrality, distanced impartiality, reflection, and lucidity; those of the German "genius," metaphysical sentiment, spiritual commitment, action, and sincerity. Interestingly enough, Goethe, as an individual author, manages for de Man to combine the seemingly opposed elements of both sides, whereas the Flemish, as a national group, stand more or less midway between the two. It is probably not surprising that the Germans tend to come off somewhat better in these comparisons than the French. Indeed, if one takes the qualities attributed to the

French and then adds to them two more, decadence and the cold-blooded self-glorification of the mediocre, one gets the makeup of the third group characterized in these articles, the Jews. No wonder, then, that Derrida, both Jewish and French yet staunchly loyal to his colleague and friend, should find writing about de Man in the aftermath of these revelations so deeply distressing a task.

In these articles, the assertion of totalizing national and racial identities is coupled with regular reference to another sort of totalizing force, that of the evolutionary "laws" of political, social, and economic development. It is the forward motion of this development, in the thought of several of the writers de Man selects for discussion, that makes such phenomena as the workings of "Hitlerism" in and through the German spirit (in the course of the current "revolution") and the growing hegemony of Germany throughout Europe seem inevitable. The power of these "laws," moreover, is such that it may well make the politics of collaboration, as a practical issue, neither right nor wrong but unavoidable — and thus unquestionable for the people of Europe caught up in the ongoing "flow" of history.

Literature, too, is described as following great evolutionary laws, but both its laws and their effects are definitely distinct from those of the political and economic spheres. The realm of literature and literary development is of course affected by sociopolitical developments (thus rendering unthinkable, for example, any immediate return to the "lost paradise" of apolitical intellectual and aesthetic circles in the Parisian 1920's and early 1930's), but poetics in its state of semiautonomy has enough of a life of its own, in terms of both literary tradition and contemporary literary development, that it remains neither coincident with nor subservient to other social and moral phenomena. This special difference is one of the reasons why de Man can implicitly adhere to more or less standard notions of literary canons, aesthetic beauty, and "eternal" poetic truth even while openly championing figures and movements that, though seemingly marginal or aberrant, he regards as vital, such as Joyce, Kafka, Lawrence, the symbolists, Paul Eluard, the surrealists, and the group formed around the Parisian journal *Messages*. This difference also explains in part the admiration de

Man expresses for the imaginative intensity and the persistence of Charles Péguy, the brilliant "Dreyfusard" whose situation, as Derrida notes,[7] seemed to share a good many circumstances with de Man's own.

Before moving from consideration of these articles, two in particular deserve further discussion, each of them significant in its own right and each instructive for what it shows about the principal elements of de Man's thought, as described above, during this period. Both of the articles in question appeared in *Le Soir*, one in the spring of 1941, the other in early 1942. The first, "Les Juifs dans la littérature actuelle" ("The Jews in Contemporary Literature"), is by far the most notorious of the articles made available in advance of their publication in volume, while the second, "Paul Valéry et la poésie symboliste" ("Paul Valéry and Symbolist Poetry"), is the most single-mindedly "literary."[8] In the often-discussed article on the role that Jews have played in contemporary literature, de Man explains the relatively minor significance of that role by utilizing both the scheme of racial characteristics and the grand evolutionary laws that appear here and elsewhere in these essays. It is true, according to de Man, that the Jews have played a substantial part in the contrived and disordered life throughout Europe since 1920, and it is also true that the Jews themselves have contributed to spreading the myth of their importance in specifically literary matters; but in terms of literature, de Man claims, "the reality is different." The inward psychological focus of the modern novel, far from being the result merely of recent social chaos or of typically Jewish cerebrality and analytic lucidity, is on the contrary nothing but the continuation and the deepening of the aesthetics of classical realism, already well over a century old. The same sort of argument, mutatis mutandis, can be made for the development of poetry, with seemingly revolutionary movements as surrealism and futurism deriving from strong and salutary poetic antecedents. Indeed, by taking the long view of literary development, one can see that the evidence that contemporary literature has remained thoroughly healthy, free from the influence of a "foreign force," proves the vitality of the literary tradition itself. It is from this viewpoint on the salubrious condition of modern letters that de Man, in conclusion, comments on the proposal for establishing an isolated colony made up of European Jews, a proposal that, to his mind, would in no respect harm the literature of the West. Although this piece has drawn a large measure of criticism for its anti-Semitic thrust — a thrust that, by any lights, is undeniable — it is of at least equal moment for the way it encapsulates (while in fact arguing against what de Man terms "vulgar anti-Semitism") the major tenets of de Man's thought and the standard formulae of his rhetoric operating throughout these articles.[9]

The essay on Valéry is a different sort of piece. Whereas the totalizing force of de Man's thought remains in evidence — a force that creates precisely the kinds of totality that de Man's later work will strive so assiduously to undo — its objects are remarkably distinct from those of the other articles. In this instance, de Man's writing reflects two forms of total, overriding presence: on the one hand the presence of the imposing figure of the great poet, on the other the presence of speech itself. It is impossible to do justice to the complexity and the depth of this essay in a brief paragraph or two. It should be said, however, by way of introduction, that this is one of the pieces that demonstrate how deeply de Man had thought about literary meaning and literary form even at this early stage of his life as a critic. The "pretext" of the article is an interview (of which only a few traces actually appear in the text) following one of Valéry's public lectures. In essence, the article is a defense by de Man against the charge that Valéry, along with the other symbolists, attempted to reduce the world to poetic form, thus effectively leaving behind the world of matter and sense — and so, of human society — in order to enclose the truth of existence in the artifice of poetic creation.

The defense of Valéry's poetry runs more or less simultaneously along two lines, the first having to do with the *desire* behind poetic creation, the second with the *means* of poetic expression. Valéry, for his part, explains in regard to his poetic production that, if he had it all to do over again, he would try to include in his verse a "global aspect" of the human spirit in order to suggest the "complete possibilities" of human knowledge and awareness. So the problem is not one of Valéry's ambitions or desires as a poet but rather one inherent in the medium of poetic expression, the "tool" of language, which, as Valéry laments, and de Man with him, is utterly inadequate to the task at hand. Whether the problem is located *within* linguistic tradition, in the conceptual roots of the words of poetry, or in the always impure relationship between poetry and the world *without*, between words and things, what de Man terms the "capricious instrument" of poetic language is never (unlike painting or music) equal to the artistic challenge, can never, in terms of poetic form, furnish the proper and "worthy" recipient for poetry's "infinitely precious content," its spiritual beauty and spiritual truth. Because of the precious value of poetry's prize, however, Valéry's poetic endeavors do not cease, and this regardless of the drama of creative anguish in which de Man's presentation of Valéry's efforts is cast (indeed, in this short six-paragraph article, one form or another of the word "anguish" recurs three times in the last three paragraphs).

In certain important respects, then, this piece seems a foreshortened precursor of de Man's mature work. Despite the fact that his later works contain very little extended discussion of Valéry, many of the hallmarks of de Manian deconstruction are already apparent here: the struggle between figural and literal meanings of language (here artistic and worldly), the insistence on intellectual doubt as the crucial attitude of all rigorous thought, the inevitable duplicity of language as the essential yet irremediably flawed medium of human thought and expression, and the crisis of anxiety that the perception of such problems repeatedly evokes. In fact, these issues, when couched in the terms of responsibility and guilt underlying the hypostatized accusations against Valéry and de Man's consequent defense, recall in their broad configurations the central issues at stake in de Man's 1977 essay on Rousseau's *Confessions*, one of de Man's best-known essays and one that has received a great deal of attention in the aftermath of the "scandal."

Nevertheless, it is necessary at this point to recall the two versions of overriding presence with which we began, each of which serves to tie this piece to de Man's other early articles and to differentiate it from his later work. In the article on Valéry, de Man's attitude toward the individual is quite distant from the thoroughgoing deconstruction of the metaphor of the self, of the unified individual subject, that is so consistent in his later writings. True, de Man begins the article by commenting on the occasional disparity between the character of an author as hypothesized by his readers and the actual nature of the man as he appears in flesh and blood. But the emphasis in this context is not on difference or absence but on presence, in the form of the "extraordinary charm" and the "irresistible, captivating" personality of the great artist. The power of Valéry's personal presence is augmented by the energetic force of his speech, as embodied in de Man's repeated reference to Valéry's affirmations in conversation, above all in the "private conversation" granted to de Man as an interviewer for *Le Soir*. So if this article assumes some of the same positions as do the later works of de Man, it nonetheless adopts them only halfway. Like so many of these early pieces *and* so many of de Man's later essays, it treats questions of authority, language, worldly reference, spiritual qualities, and truth, while not yet leaving behind completely the totalizing tendencies of de Man's early thought to move into the realm of anguished uncertainty and undecidability of his mature works. Again, it seems particularly fitting that an article on Valéry — who, as de Man himself notes, acted as a link between the earlier symbolists and the subsequent poets of the twentieth century — should furnish the midpoint, albeit in a minor key, between the early and the later de Man, and particularly regrettable that de Man did not return to Valéry for extended discussion in his later years.

Given de Man's lengthy silence regarding these early articles, and the rigorous critique of totalizing thought in his later works,[10] it is possible to regard de Man's behavior, as does Geoffrey Hartman, for example, as a sign of de Man's eventual disenchantment with the rhetoric of totalitarianism and with the "fatal aestheticizing of politics" that "gave fascism its false brilliance."[11] It is also possible not only to argue for the potentially disruptive elements of de Man's early thought (as Derrida does in part, including reference to a French Resistance volume entitled *Exercise du silence*, the publication of which was perhaps aided by de Man) but also to argue, as Derrida does, too, for the politically subversive nature of all genuinely deconstructive thought.[12] Each of these issues has received notable attention in the period since de Graef's discovery. Nonetheless, in the world of academe, as opposed to that of the general public, and in particular in the area of academics closest to de Man, neither the politics of de Man's early writings nor the politics of deconstruction per se — about both of which I admit to being skeptical in the extreme — have really been, up to now, at the center of debate. Rather, that center has been constituted by the deeply personalized reactions of a large number of academic critics to the memory of de Man as a teacher and colleague and/or to de Man's work as an active influence and as an example, whether one to be diligently followed or thoroughly rejected. This highly charged center of debate, along with the very personal nature of the reactions by those who knew or read de Man, accounts to a large extent for the oddly skewed and patently agonized defenses, attacks, and counterattacks that have been a significant part of academic publications and conferences on de Man's wartime activities. In the long run, it may well be that the reactions to the de Man revelations will turn out to be more significant, and ultimately more disturbing, than anything that came to light in the course of the disclosures themselves.

I would like to suggest why it may be that these reactions have been so confused and, in many instances, so fraught with pain. What I have to say deals primarily with those who were students and close colleagues of de Man, who knew him and conversed with him and heard him lecture, but the substance of these remarks also applies, I believe, to those who did not know the man but only his work, because the subject matter and the effect of his writing were more or less the same as those of his teaching, and the tone of his essays was very similar to the tone he would adopt in seminars or lectures: authoritative, intellectually engaging, rigorously logical (if also, at key points, disconcertingly elliptical), and utterly self-assured. It is not difficult to perceive that this voice, the unquestioned authority and self-assurance of which have often subsequently been acknowledged by de Man's students, runs exactly contrary to the subject matter of de Manian deconstruction, to the assertions of inadequacy, uncertainty, and rigorously conceived undecidability of meaning and the ways in which meaning is played out in the world, whether in language, history, literature, or other spheres. Indeed, when Derrida speaks of the "many contradictory lessons"[13] of the whole affair, de Man's own critical and pedagogical practice may well be already inscribed within those very contradictions.

Turning for a moment to Freud's later work, specifically to *Beyond the Pleasure Principle* (1920), it is germane here to recall that in Freud's concept of the instincts — and there is no scenario more suited to the Freudian drama of the instincts than the pedagogical one — the individual subject may be stimulated by the sudden loss of a stable center, but such stimulation will be prolonged in the guise of lasting pleasure if and only if stability can be recaptured, preferably through the willful action of the individual in question. This stability and this center, so thoroughly undercut by the message of de Man's discourse, were in practice regularly reestablished within the same scene, reinvested in the authoritative voice of the master himself. This is one reason why so many of de Man's students and colleagues, in some cases irrespective of their own gifts as critics or their propensities for various aspects of literary interpretation, imitated de Man to such an extraordinary degree both in their choice of topics and in their treatment of those topics.

None of this so far seems astounding or even very noteworthy — teachers have been teaching and students learning in much the same way for centuries. But in the case of de Man, two further elements combined to make matters considerably more complex than even a specialized sort of intellectual hero-worship would explain: de Man's extended exercise of silence and his untimely death. That de Man began publishing books relatively late in life (the first edition of *Blindness and Insight* dates to 1971) made his death in 1983, due to inoperable cancer, seem all the more premature. It does not require a very careful reading of Freud's "Mourning and Melancholia" to perceive that the normal process of mourning on the part of all those close to him in the academic community, a process seemingly complete, was oddly revivified by the sudden revelation of de Man's activities and his silence about them, as though de Man, but now somehow significantly different, had been brought back to life only to suffer another death, this time one that abrogated mourning as such and instituted in its place something that was neither mourning nor melancholy alone but both, with a good measure of doubt and uncertainty added in.

This grief, however, was compounded by what for de Man, in his practice as a teacher and critic, had been another kind of silence. Derrida touches briefly on this point at the opening of his essay in *Critical Inquiry* when he says, "even for his admirers and his friends, especially for them, if I may be allowed to testify to this, *the work and the person* of Paul de Man were enigmatic."[14] In seminars de Man was always, as I have mentioned, intellectually engaging and engaged, but he was also, in terms of affect, personally withdrawn, tending not toward the reassurances of unnecessary or superfluous speech but instead toward silence. This often enigmatic silence, in the scene of pedagogy and conversation, could be and was filled in by his listeners and interlocutors, perhaps to a far greater extent than he himself could have realized or would have sanctioned. At any rate, the sort of Freudian transference, however oblique or partial, that this procedure invited (a procedure mirrored in a way by the conspicuous ellipses in de Man's writing) eventually resulted in one of the most emotionally embattled debates in American literary studies in this century. It is undeniable that the irony of this situation has been especially cruel for those of de Man's students and colleagues who happened to be Jewish. But the overall problem is, it seems to me, broader and, for many, more immediate than the single issue of anti-Semiticism, since it has to do with a still more universal question, that of mourning, and more specifically, how to mourn the figure of a lost father who comes back to life not as a father or even as an uncle but as someone else altogether, almost a total stranger.

At the same time, given the mixture of doubling and victimage in the course of these revelations and the debate over them, the proper framework of analysis — for the deeply divided reactions of the American academic community overall as well as for the spectacle presented by the popular press — may finally be Girardian rather than just Freudian. For American academics, it is significant, from a Girardian perspective on the disorder of all sacrificial crises, that the de Man revelations came at a time of remarkable confusion in American theoretical positions, a confusion that has proceeded through various phases since the decline of the New Criticism in the 1950's. In this same vein, it is noteworthy that Hayden White, in his blurb for Frank Lentricchia's *After the New Criticism* (1980), describes the current plethora of positions and counterpositions in the United States as "the 'civil war' . . . raging in American literary-critical theory." Regarding the victimization of de Man in the American press, the exemplary article is David Lehman's 1988 piece in *Newsweek*, which likens deconstruction to "the thousand-year Reich" and is accompanied by a telling pair of photographs: a well-known picture of de Man, smiling, seated in front of a shelf of books, and a photo of storm troopers holding swastikas and marching beneath a huge banner that displays the Reich's emblem.[15] It is not surprising that academic authors like Derrida and Miller were so upset with the snowballing publicity that the entire matter received once the press got hold of it, since the publishing avenues of academic explication and "defense" are so much slower. By the time any sort of thoroughgoing rational explanation or discussion could appear — even taking into account the three- or four-month "blackout" imposed by deconstruction's proponents in the late summer and fall of 1987 — the press had already arrived at its judgment without any recourse to legalistic trials, a judgment it disseminated, in true ritualistic fashion, rapidly and without pity for any of those involved. Perhaps ironically, but completely understandably in a Girardian sense, the more that the academic critics said and wrote in the course of the scandal — in the end regardless of whether their words were friendly or unfriendly to de Man — the more they found themselves contributing, like it or not, to this ritualistic process. We are still, in literary studies in the United States at least, in the throes of this trauma, and I fear we will not find ourselves completely free of it any time soon. We can only hope that the experience will teach us something about the dangers of the aestheticization of politics — about which, in any case, we should have already been well instructed by Benjamin, Gramsci, and others — and also something more about that most difficult of ideological authorities to deny, to destroy, *or* to manage, the elusive yet ever-present intellectual and affective entity of the *sujet supposé savoir*.

In the end, I do not believe it is possible to argue, though some attempted to do so in the wake of the scandal, that deconstruction *itself* is necessarily political — either politically conservative or politically revolutionary. Nonetheless, even while highlighting uncertainty and fragmentation as opposed to stable knowledge and totality in a strictly academic environment, American deconstruction has left authoritarian totality alone to function in the world as practical oppression despite the theoretical undoing of authoritarianism's mandates and its aims. De Man's early writings often stressed and at times lauded various forms of totalizing thought; his mature writings broke such forms apart (even to the point of retreating from his own projected study of the history of rhetoric suggested at several points in the 1970's). There *is* a link between these two differing periods in de Man's critical production, however, even if that link consists only in programmatic blindness, denial, and silence. That the other connection, the relation between the absence and the presence of totalizing authority, has to do, in this instance, with the voice of the master in the scene of pedagogy remains important more for the way in which the scandal was played out in de Man's posthumous audience than for the evaluation of his work itself. Both sorts of projects, study of de Man's critical corpus in its entirety and study of the turbulent reactions to the revelations of 1987, seem to me to require much further investigation before we will have a genuine understanding of what de Man wrote and of what his writings *in toto*, once given an uncannily renewed life of their own, actually did and continue to do. Painful as it may be, this is work that must now be undertaken, and it may well prove to be the most lasting legacy of Paul de Man's silences.

11

"Against Theory?" Yes and No

AMONG THE ONGOING debates in literary theory in the United States, one of the more spirited has been that known by the catchphrase "Against Theory." Unlike controversies that draw their inspiration either from European thought, in particular Heideggerean, Derridean, or even post-Crocean continental philosophy, or from recently defined intellectual movements in the United States, such as contemporary feminism or cultural studies, the positions and counterpositions taken up in the discussion "for" and "against" theory have their roots firmly planted in nineteenth-century American philosophical tradition, especially in the pragmatism of William James and C. S. Peirce, in part as interpreted and refashioned by such "new pragmatists" as Richard Rorty, Donald Davidson, and Stanley Fish. Indeed, the subtitle of the volume of essays on this topic reads: "Literary Studies and the New Pragmatism."[1] If these roots limit the entire matter a good deal more than the first part of the subtitle may imply — limit it, that is, to a discussion of "literary studies" having to do primarily with J. L. Austin, W. V. O. Quine, Noam Chomsky, and related Anglo-American philosophies of language — nonetheless, the implications of this debate are far-reaching not only within this philosophical tradition but within literary hermeneutics as a whole. The "Against Theory" debate is also noteworthy, moreover, for what it shows about the rising skepticism in the United States not just toward the sort of "theory" treated in *Against Theory* but also toward literary theory in general (a skepticism that appeared with equal force, though in somewhat different manner, in the scandal over the wartime writings of Paul de Man).

So far, the bibliography of the debate has been fairly easy to trace. It began with a baker's dozen of essays originally published in *Critical Inquiry*, collected and republished in the volume *Against Theory* in 1985 by W. J. T. Mitchell, editor of *Critical Inquiry*, who also provided an introduction. The essays include the eponymous opening shot of 1982 by Steven Knapp and Walter Benn Michaels; a series of comments, objections, and queries by Daniel T. O'Hara, E. D. Hirsch, Jonathan Crewe, Steven Mailloux, Hershel Parker, Adena Rosmarin, William C. Dowling, Stanley Fish, and Richard Rorty; and two further "Replies" by Knapp and Michaels. To date, there has been one further follow-up by Knapp and Michaels ("Against Theory 2"), and a number of reviews and articles have appeared in other journals with similar interests.[2]

From the start, Knapp and Michaels's 1982 essay "Against Theory" takes as its target a concisely defined area of critical activity: "By 'theory' we mean a special project in literary criticism: the attempt to govern interpretations of particular texts by appealing to an account of interpretation in general" (AT, p. 11). This remarkably narrow definition of literary theory turns out eventually to be crucial to the success of the authors' argument. But before discussing the limitations of Knapp and Michaels's work, we should note that this opening description of their subject proclaims both what, in their view, theory is and what theory is not. Theory *is* any endeavor to stand outside of the practical analysis of literary texts in order to "govern" — control, force, prescribe — interpretation by appeal to an overarching interpretive theory that would hold in any and all cases. Theory *is not* such "essentially, empirical" and thus nontheoretical and noninterpretive subjects as narratology, stylistics, and prosody, to say nothing of theories of inspiration, genre, reception, and so forth. According to Knapp and Michaels, the distinctive strategy of the sort of theory they are dealing with, as well as theory's persistent error, consists in "splitting apart terms that are in fact inseparable" (p. 12). Because theory characteristically generates its inquiry by selecting a *pair* of notions — meaning and intention, language and speech acts, knowledge and belief — and then attempting to explain one of them by appeal to the other, which is to say by *grounding* one term in the authority of the other, the entire endeavor folds when it is seen that the two notions in question are indeed not two but one, that they never should have been separated in the first place.

Knapp and Michaels are clearest on this point in their introductory remarks about the recurrent debates on the relation between authorial intention and the meaning of texts. Although some theorists, like Hirsch and P. D. Juhl, claim that correct interpretations depend on an appeal to authorial intention, while others, like Paul de Man, assume that by denying the possibility of recovering stable authorial intention they also deny the possibility of positive, valid interpretations, the differences in these perspectives are not nearly so significant as the underlying similarity, which is the mistaken assumption that meaning and intention are separable entities:

> Once it is seen that the meaning of a text is simply identical to the author's intended meaning, the project of *grounding* meaning in intention becomes incoherent. Since the project itself is incoherent, it can neither succeed nor fail; hence both theoretical attitudes toward intention are irrelevant. The mistake made by theorists has been to imagine the possibility or desirability of moving from one term (the author's intended meaning) to a second term (the text's meaning), when actually the two terms are the same. One can neither succeed nor fail in deriving one term from the other, since to have one is already to have them both. (AT, p. 12)

For Knapp and Michaels, then, as Mitchell says in his introduction, "interpretation, the finding of meaning just *is* the finding of intention" (AT, p. 5), nothing more and nothing less.

At this juncture it should be pointed out that despite the narrowness of Knapp and Michaels's definition of theory, their intended critique, within the limits they set, is extraordinarily thoroughgoing, having to do not so much with a special way of "doing theory" as with the typical ways in which theories "always go wrong" (AT, p. 12) and, finally, with "the idea of doing theory at all" (p. 11). The authors end their brief introduction with a description of their own essayistic strategies, a proleptic conclusion, and then a recommendation that is no less than startling: "Our examples are meant to represent the central mechanism of all theoretical arguments, and our treatment of them is meant to indicate that all such arguments will fail and fail in the same way. If we are right, then the whole enterprise of critical theory is misguided *and should be abandoned*" (p. 12, my italics).

In the succeeding pages, Knapp and Michaels discuss two "ontological" issues (the relation between intention and meaning and that between language and speech acts) and one "epistemological" issue (the relation between knowledge and what they term "true belief") in order to show in every case that there is no "relation" at all since in reality each pair of terms collapses into one. To make a short story shorter still, there is for Knapp and Michaels no such thing as intentionless meaning, any more than there is beliefless knowledge or human language in the absence of speech acts. For example, "language" that is truly without intention is also without meaning and therefore is not actually language but merely a set of bogus "signs" that happen to *resemble* real signs. Regarding the various pairs of distinctions and the various methods of interpretation that such distinctions themselves would invite, there is not a genuine choice or even a genuine range of choice but only a range of error.

To make this argument, and to reassert the claim that a text has only one meaning and that its meaning is whatever its author intends (an assertion reiterated ever more trenchantly in the course of Knapp and Michaels's successive essays), the authors offer what can only be termed a practical example, an account of a poem seemingly left "written" in the sand by the motions of the waves on a beach. The treatment of the wave poem, Wordsworth's "A Slumber Did My Spirit Seal," provides one of the essay's more fanciful moments as well as its single gesture, albeit a weak one, toward anything like critical practice. The authors discuss, in narrative order, the possibilities for understanding this apparent linguistic phenomenon that a casual observer might run through: the squiggles are produced randomly by the operation of the waves (perhaps aided by "erosion, percolation, etc.," AT, pp. 15–16) and are therefore meaningless, their resemblance to language and specifically to the stanzas of Wordsworth's poem being merely — if also uncannily — coincidental; or the sea itself is alive and is expressing pantheistic sentiments; or Wordsworth lives on as a hidden genius of the shore, slyly repeating his favorite lyrics. Although the list of possibilities could be expanded ad infinitum, the functional options offered by Knapp and Michaels are exactly two. Either the poem as written does not express any intention by any conscious agent whatsoever and is therefore not language, or it expresses authorial intention and therefore is language and is, thus, interpretable. In a strange coda to this scene, the authors further refine their schema of possibilities by introducing a small submarine filled with men in white coats who appear to be experimenting with the effects of some underwater writing device. But the principal format — no intention, thus no meaning; intention, thus meaning — remains basically unchanged.

It is true that the entire recounted episode, occurring as it does in the midst of otherwise lucid and crisply straightforward exposition, appears at best "quaint."[3] But the problems the episode opens up in terms of intention, meaning, and interpretation cut far deeper than such a description implies. Some of these problems have been elucidated by Peggy Kamuf in a review article.[4] Kamuf begins by pointing out a certain semantic imprecision in the various ways Knapp and Michaels adopt the term "author." By using the notions of citation and iterability as well as the Derridean (but also Husserlian) distinction between finite and general linguistic intention, Kamuf goes on to suggest that, in one regard, Knapp and Michaels's demonstration that the scientists chose to reproduce Wordsworth's poem results in a strange "authorial" possibility indeed: that the meaning of "A Slumber Did My Spirit Seal," as found on the beach, is simply that a bunch of white-coated scientists wanted (intended) to see if their new-fangled gadget would work. So much for the suggestive richness of lyric poetry.

Along an even broader front, Kamuf takes the authors of

"Against Theory" to task for skimming over, in the "all-or-nothing" logic of their empiricism, the complex questions within the notion of intentionality that Derrida raised in his well-known exchange on this topic with John Searle.[5] As a final gambit, Kamuf produces a reading of Knapp and Michaels's "fable" of the wave poem that indicates the surprising extent to which Knapp and Michaels, while studiously attempting to avoid developing their own practical reading of Wordsworth's poem, end up getting trapped both in the poem's rhetorical strategies and in the import of its thematics. The "now" of the poem and the insistent series of "nows" in Knapp and Michaels's narrative combine to raise the question of "then," of the present/absent author and speaker of both of these literary "pieces" as well as of the thematics of death and, perhaps, spectral rebirth in and through discourse. Though it could also be said that Kamuf herself, in her argumentative strategies and in her citations, falls into the same trap of "undecidable" reiteration — with respect to such figures as de Man, Derrida, J. Hillis Miller, Harold Bloom, and perhaps Barbara Johnson — that Knapp and Michaels fall into with respect to Wordsworth, the fundamental question she raises, in a literary *and* a critical sense, continues in force: who speaks? The mere broaching of this question recalls the multiple strains of philosophical and literary inquiry into the nature of authorship, intentionality, and literary tradition from the nineteenth century on into the twentieth (one thinks immediately of Mallarmé and Nietzsche, but also of Flaubert, D'Annunzio, Pirandello, Joyce, and Faulkner), about which Knapp and Michaels seem to have barely an inkling.

Before returning to the way the argument develops in "Against Theory," we should note that one of the problems giving rise to Kamuf's objection concerning the interpretation of the wave poem, the problem of incremental or alternating meaning as opposed to fixed or stable meaning, is cleared up by Knapp and Michaels in their 1987 article, "Against Theory 2."[6] In the latter essay, Knapp and Michaels assert in the strongest terms possible not only that the meaning of a text is what its *historical* author intended but also that a text "has only *one* meaning, and that whatever that meaning is, it *never* changes" (AT2, p. 68, my italics). This assertion does not, it is true, so much address the problems of reiteration and citation implicit in the story of the wave poem as simply close off such questions as potential difficulties. Nevertheless, it does establish Knapp and Michaels's position in this respect (creating at the same time, however, an equally insidious problem in their notion of "history," since any conception of the "historical author" that would still include even the case that "the historical author is the universal muse" does not augur well for historical investigation, empirical or otherwise).[7]

Prior to Knapp and Michaels's discussion of the wave poem, the principal theorist treated in "Against Theory" had been Hirsch, whereas in later sections the authors train their sights on de Man and Fish. In Knapp and Michaels's view, all three critics (along with Juhl)[8] commit the characteristic errors of the theorist; that is, they separate terms that should not be separated and ground one through an appeal to the authority of the other. At first glance, Hirsch and Fish might seem odd choices for the authors to have made in selecting opponents, since Hirsch's intentionalism and Fish's antifoundationalism both inform major aspects of Knapp and Michaels's position. But even though the authors are perfectly willing to admit such influences, their disagreements with Hirsch and Fish continue unabated because, while both Hirsch and Fish *would* be correct *if* they rigorously followed their arguments to their seemingly ineluctable conclusions, neither theorist has really understood what in each instance Knapp and Michaels term the "force" of his own thought (AT, pp. 13, 27). Hirsch, on this account, separates meaning and intention almost in spite of himself in order to get his theorizing going. In doing so, according to Knapp and Michaels, Hirsch envisions a time of interpretive indeterminacy in language and then *adds* authorial intention to language in order to get meaning (a description with which, in regard both to its temporalization and to its point, Hirsch himself disagrees: *AT,* pp. 49–50). Fish, in like manner and with like results, separates knowledge and belief even while attempting to mix them back together again.

A considerably more interesting and more challenging case would have been furnished by de Man's work. But the authors have very little to say about de Man beyond the single basic assertion, apropos of his 1977 essay on Rousseau's *Confessions*, that de Man takes the position that language is essentially arbitrary and inherently meaningless, the "negative" position discussed by Knapp and Michaels as that which considers intention as something to be "subtracted from" texts in order to get at whatever it is that textual meaning is all about (AT, pp. 21–24). In Knapp and Michaels's scheme, this position fully contrasts with that of such "positive" critics as Hirsch and Juhl and at least half contrasts with the position of W. K. Wimsatt, Jr., and Monroe C. Beardsley as set forth in Wimsatt and Beardsley's famous New Critical treatise, the formalist grandfather of all modern discussions of intentionality in literary criticism, "The Intentional Fallacy."[9]

In Knapp and Michaels's reprise of 1987, "Against Theory 2," they expand their critique of theoretical positions to hermeneutics, especially the thought of Paul Ricoeur and Hans-Georg Gadamer, and deconstruction, especially that of Derrida. Knapp and Michaels argue against each of these latter interpretive positions by sticking to a strict intentionalist stance. Hermeneutics is thus in error when assuming that a text not only means "what its author intends but also necessarily means more, acquiring new meanings as readers apply it to new situations"; and deconstruction is in error when assuming that an individual author "can never succeed in determining the meaning of a text, [that] every text participates in a code that necessarily eludes authorial control" (AT2, p. 50). In countering both of these forms of "weak conventionalism" (in a procedure seen by the authors as complementary to their earlier attack on forms of "strong conventionalism"), Knapp and Michaels assert that conventions do not provide either a source for or a determining influence on the meaning of the text but only evidence of what that meaning (already) is, which, of course, is a matter of intention rather than convention. As Knapp and Michaels state in their overtly polemical conclusion:

Conventions provide no source of meaning in addition to intention . . . [and] they impose no necessary constraint on how intentions can be expressed. They provide no additional source and they impose no necessary constraints because their role is not to determine a text's meaning but only to provide evidence of what the text's meaning is. And its meaning is whatever its author intends. (AT2, p. 68)

This essay expands the critical horizons of the earlier one both by considering such competing interpretive strategies as historical hermeneutics and deconstruction and by actively engaging questions of legal theory (currently a topic of heated debate in the United States, although in their treatment of it the authors clearly remain literary critics rather than the general theorists they had seemed to become in the penultimate paragraph of their 1983 "Reply"). The essay also clarifies Knapp and Michaels's earlier distinctions between convention and intention while adding a further one between interpreting and creating—that is, uncovering or locating original meaning as opposed to producing new meaning. But the 1987 essay does not change the essential message expressed in the initial "Against Theory" and reaffirmed in the authors' subsequent replies to the critics of that essay. I have already touched on most of the salient elements of that message, but there remains one aspect of Knapp and Michaels's position in regard to theory that should be mentioned. This aspect, stressed by Knapp and Michaels in their conclusion to the initial "Against Theory," has to do with the vexed question of the relation between critical theory and critical practice. Although it would perhaps have been easiest for the authors to affirm in the end that theory and practice are merely another pair of separated entities that should not be separated and that theory, therefore, is just another form of practice, this is not at all the tack they take. For Knapp and Michaels, theory is not simply a kind of harmless logical aberration but, as they say from the outset, a plague on the land that demands a cure. On this topic, it is only fitting to let Knapp and Michaels have the last word:

The theoretical impulse, as we have described it, always involves the attempt to separate things that should not be separated. . . . It is tempting to end by saying that theory and practice too are inseparable. But this would be a mistake. Not because theory and practice . . . really are separate but because theory is nothing else but the attempt to escape practice. Meaning is just another name for expressed intention, knowledge just another name for true belief, but theory is not just another name for practice. It is the name for all the ways people have tried to stand outside practice in order to govern practice from without. Our thesis has been that no one can reach a position outside practice, that theorists should stop trying, and that the theoretical enterprise should therefore come to an end. (AT, pp. 29–30)

Some of the commentaries on Knapp and Michaels's essay that are included in the volume *Against Theory* are significant. Two sorts of objections concerning literary history come up now and again. First, Knapp and Michaels's point of view may well tend to discourage broadly based historical scholarship: since searching for meaning as authorial intention might already appear to be a historical project, literary history that is not author-centered as an object of study will seemingly take care of itself. Second, Knapp and Michaels's own work betrays a dismaying ignorance of the history of theory, about which they appear informed only as regards the last two centuries or so and only in the Anglo-American tradition. Crewe, O'Hara, and Rorty voice concerns about the "professional" (at times "careerist") implications of Knapp and Michaels's opinions. Hirsch, Mailloux, Rosmarin, and Dowling all raise points of theoretical interest, as does Parker, who stands aside from the other writers here (with the partial exception of Hirsch) in bringing up the perturbing implications that textual criticism would have had for Knapp and Michaels's argument had they cared to consider it.

Along with such commentary, *Against Theory* also includes an extension of the positions taken in "Against Theory" in the form of Fish's essay, coyly entitled "Consequences" (*AT*, pp. 106–31). Fish's contention, which is maintained not only in Knapp and Michaels's essay but also throughout Fish's own *Is There a Text in This Class?*,[10] is that theory has no practical consequences of any import whatever. It is true, Fish concedes toward the end of "Consequences," that theory has entered the academic marketplace, that it is taught and written and written about. But, Fish declares in an argument familiar by now to all of his readers, the sort of consequences "theory" has are not only within practice but, of necessity, utterly subservient to practice, with the result that the consequences that are *denied* to theory — the possibility of gaining a purchase outside practice to govern it from without — are in fact "the only consequences that matter" (*AT*, p. 125).

In terms of the volume *Against Theory*, then, Knapp and Michaels seem to have carried the day. The collection does contain one genuine attack, however disjointed, by O'Hara, as well as some quibbling and a few border skirmishes of note (Crewe on the profession; Dowling on formalism and the mutual entailment, as opposed to identity, of meaning and intention; Rorty on pragmatist philosophy). But generally speaking both the *critical categories* established by Knapp and Michaels and the *overall approach* they take in treating those categories remain unchallenged. In one sense, of course, this sort of basic unanimity is heartening. Still, one wonders, in a volume introduced as the embodiment of a controversial and important debate, just what such consensus really shows. More specifically, it may seem that the argument of "Against Theory" — for all the spirited glibness of its presentation, its rhetorical self-assurance and invective (what Kamuf characterizes as the rhetorical "scare tactic" of intimidation),[11] and its marked tendency to stipulate or assert its most fundamental points rather than to demonstrate or argue them — only works because the essay's authors are perfectly well aware of preaching to, and only to, the converted (which is perhaps why, in the end, there is no real response from Knapp and Michaels to Parker's textual/historical examples).

Does this mean then that there can be no pertinent criticism of Knapp and Michaels from within the orbit of concerns they themselves describe? Hardly. By way of conclusion, I would like, first, to make a very broad observation about why their project seems on the face of it to work so well in warding off objections and, second, to pose a brief series of questions that the project itself raises without supplying, or even attempting to supply, satisfactory answers. The observation, which has more to do with the limits of Knapp and Michaels's project than might at first appear to be the case, is that absolute intentionalism works absolutely. That is, once it is given that literary meaning and authorial intention are absolutely the same thing, and that every genuine interpretive practice is thus aimed at this phenomenon whether consciously or unconsciously, it is not difficult to see that every other supposed goal — or hindrance — of any interpretive program will prove to be aberrant, wrong, incoherent, and so forth. The trouble is — and Knapp and Michaels obviously sense this in stating that their position has no effect whatever on critical practice — that this "given" is so limiting as to render the proposition itself either circular, mundane, or both. Knapp and Michaels's interpretive machine, once set in motion, always works: but if it always works, what is so interesting about it? Indeed, the inevitable suspicion is that it always works because its design is to steer clear of what would be the authentically interesting questions regarding meaning, intention, criticism, theory, and interpretation rather than to address such questions in a nonpolemical, "nonstipulative" way. Samuel Weber, in a commentary on Stanley Fish that is germane in this context,[12] puts his finger on one of the argumentative strategies that has stood Fish in good stead over the years, one that Knapp and Michaels would appear to have learned well: the strategy of setting up limits to the field of debate (tacitly or not) and then working within those limits as though the issues at stake were not limited at all, as though the bounds of concern, once determined, were invisible even while remaining absolutely in force, much as, for example, a tempest in a teapot must seem for the tea. This is not to say that what is at stake in the debate for and against "theory" is necessarily of the nature of such a tempest — in fact these issues are far more important and more pressing than that — but only that the authors' conception of their topic and their manner of presenting it, even while guaranteeing the success of their position, do so at the cost of avoiding the more far-reaching questions that their work would otherwise naturally raise.

It is not hard to pose at least a few of those questions. To take the most obvious one first, what is intention? True, Knapp and Michaels might answer in a single word: meaning. But the question still holds. Merely collapsing two terms by fiat into one does not *define* the combined entity: indeed, such an act *precludes* defining one in relation to the other as Knapp and Michaels so adroitly demonstrate. Nor does simply arguing against the positions of other writers provide a satisfactory definition in any explicit, positive sense. To take a related question, what is *literary* meaning? Does it include, keeping to the notion of authorial intention, conscious as well as unconscious meanings (Freudian slips, outright mistakes, and the like)? If so, to what extent are such meanings to be included in the act of interpretation? Furthermore, is literary meaning different from other kinds of meaning? Knapp and Michaels use many examples from fields as diverse as linguistics, law, philosophy, and literary criticism. Are these all really similar to literature and its tradition in terms of meaning and interpretation? Fish and Rorty might well say they are, but Fish is already steeped in the arcana of multiple-topic interpretation, and Rorty's commentary in *Against Theory* demonstrates once again that as a literary critic he is a very good philosopher. Any appeal to their work for critical authority, at least in this arena, would seem suspect at best.

Finally, and perhaps most significantly here, what is *literary* criticism and what is *literary* theory? There is little or no critical practice in Knapp and Michaels's essays on "Against Theory," so it is not easy to discern how well what they say about practice in general really corresponds to their own (or anyone else's) critical assumptions and procedures. More to the point, however, is their definition of theory, which is at least clear, if also limited. But no one today, with the possible exception of Hirsch and Fish and a handful of others, really believes that the theory of interpretation is all there is to literary theory.[13] Even if such were the case, moreover, Knapp and Michaels would have to argue their position cogently and coherently rather than simply asserting the theoretical nature of interpretation and the "essentially empirical" and so nontheoretical nature of just about everything else. Though Fish, for one, claims that the objects of the argument in "Against Theory" could easily be increased (*AT*, pp. 128–29 n. 2), it is difficult to see how such augmentation could be accomplished without utterly breaking the bounds that Knapp and Michaels's argument depends on to function as it does. All of these questions, central to discussions about literary and cultural studies in the United States and elsewhere over the past several decades, are barely grazed or are left altogether untouched by Knapp and Michaels's work. In the future, may their aim, and that of their interlocutors, be at once better and broader.

12

Weak Thought/Strong Thought

Il pensiero debole and the Problems of Postmodernity

IT WOULD BE REASSURING to conclude a study such as this with an appeal to historical unity, to the sort of unified if variegated overview of the current situation in literary criticism and theory that would cap things off in our present moment. To offer such a conclusion is a difficult task, and this for several intertwined reasons. First, our notion of history, whether capitalized à la Jameson or not, is considerably more complex in contemporary studies than it was even a few years ago, including as it did the supposedly flexible but often simply vague and almost always ethnocentrically oriented historical notions of the American "new historicism." Second, the various brands of totalizing thought that had such currency in the American academy of the 1970's and 1980's — Marxism, feminism (as distinct from gender studies), and, to almost everyone's surprise, deconstruction — have recently given over to a remarkable panoply of approaches, even "anti-approaches" (occasionally called, rather polemically, "cultural studies" to distinguish them from the earlier more conservative and highbrow conception of "intellectual history" and the apparently committed but in the end often biased concept of "cultural critique"), with the result that any gesture toward theoretical/historical totality would seem bogus on its face. Third, the very era in which we write, what I like to term the era (rather than the "moment" or the "movement" or even the "condition") of the postmodern, is one, at its best, of anti-totalizing thought both in the academy and in the world around us.

This commentary regarding intellectual flexibility, the distrust of rigid definition, and the distaste for totalities should not, however, lead to the sort of appeal to uncertainty, nondefinition, and weak-ness that would create affinities with Gianni Vattimo's idea of *il pensiero debole* ("weak thought"). Weak thought, in Vattimo's work, seems utterly unable to deal with the fundamental questions of authority or, to put it crassly, underlying strength that we con-tinue to find all around us even as we become more and more convinced that there must be a way to meld flexible systems with rigid ones, imaginative notions with analytic ones, affective critical elements and reactions with rational ones. As noted earlier in this work, one of the principal literary questions that Vattimo has been noticeably inept at approaching has been the distinction between modernism and postmodernism, and it is to that distinction that I would like to turn once again in conclusion.[1]

It seems to me fruitless to deny that there exist notable sim-ilarities, even if in the fashion of family resemblances, among the principal authors of the modernist canon in the West (say, for our present literary purposes, Pirandello, Italo Svevo, and Carlo Emilio Gadda, although Proust, the younger Joyce, and Faulkner would do as well) and among those of postmodernism (Umberto Eco, Giorgio Manganelli, and the later Italo Calvino, with the later Joyce, John Barth, and Vladimir Nabokov waiting in the wings). I believe, moreover, that there are salient differences—and not merely family differences, to belabor a term—between the two groups as groups. Although these distinctions are graded and occa-sionally obscure, they do, I repeat, exist in a significant and func-tional way, and they can be outlined, however schematically, by adopting four basic categories, to be considered one by one: au-thority, closure, alienation, and representation.

Modernist narratives appeal to interpretative authority in vari-ous ways, primarily through irony and often, as David Hayman has pointed out in his reading of Joyce's early and middle works, through the subtly ironic arrangement of narrative segments as distinct from narrative voice.[2] Along with interpretative authority, modernist texts—even as they appear open-ended—aim toward narrative closure through establishment of both moral and formal hierarchies, however provisional such hierarchies may seem at first glance. In terms of individual characters, the great theme of modernist literature, which is the relationship between the central individual and the society in which he or she (but almost always gendered as "he") lives, is portrayed in the key of distance, of individual alienation, existential uncertainty, and angst.

Finally, as regards the category of literary representation, for better or worse modernist literature believes in it, at least as a category. That is, the concern for linguistic refinement so much in evidence throughout modernist programs, the concern for prose style, regularly retained a representational format, in which the very point of actively refining narrative language was to create a fuller, more effective "portrayal" of what language was supposed to re-present outside language, be that the psychological development of the individual in the world of matter and sense or the spiritual development of human collectivity. In other words, the aesthetic model here remained one in which language, as a transparent rather than opaque agency (to borrow terminology begun by Bertrand Russell and Alfred North Whitehead), led to the world, albeit within the ever-shifting hierarchies of self-reflection and, now to follow Alfred Tarski, "meta-language."

In the literature of postmodernism, each of these categories takes on a distinctly different cast. Interpretative authority is broken apart both through fragmentation of the narrative segment and through the often-discussed effects of "citationality" woven within the narrative texture, which is now made up of a congeries of prenarrative voices all of which are on display but none of which is finally dominant or individually determinant. In the process, the modernist hierarchy of ordered narrative levels becomes flattened out into surface rather than depth, a surface now negotiable only in confusion and disarray. Narrative closure as a goal, text as product, is thus foregone in favor of the text as process. Rather than alienation, a concept that in modernist literature is linked to a notion of the individual subject, the postmodern text emphasizes the delights of process as a collective phenomenon of mass culture, as the seemingly communal immersion in the *jouissance* of post-modern appropriation and presentation. The potential closure of parody, to put this in other terms, gives over to the apparent open-endlessness of pastiche. In this way, representation, as a means of representing something outside the aesthetic experience, is abandoned as a notion, with the result that the self-contained aesthetic experience becomes the primary category of sociocultural (and I would argue also political) life, a sort of mass-cultural "games without end" at play in the world of the postmodern.

At this juncture, it would be useful to underscore a few of the problems that the above schema, at least as regards postmodernism, inevitably runs into. First, it is hard to tell exactly to what extent collective narcissism, in the era of the postmodern, means not only communal delight but also solipsism, antihistoricism, and, in effect, political withdrawal. Second, it is not at all clear that the apparent collectivity of postmodern experience is really communal rather than singular, is really an experience in which human beings are truly more "connected" or, on the other hand, is in fact one in which they are more and more alone. Third, it is undeniably true that many of the characteristics of postmodern narratives can also be found in previous works — one thinks of *Tristram Shandy* or even the *Quixote* — which makes the notion of the historical era of the postmodern one that is not absolute and that should be nuanced by prior effects of "postmodernity" in various forms of cultural expression. Finally, it is uncertain whether in the framework of the postmodern it actually makes sense, in anything other than an academic sense, to talk about literary narrative (as opposed to such other, now dominant narrative forms as television, cinema, video, and the paperback romance). However germane these problems may be, the necessary *points de repère* of any discussion of the postmodern remain in force: the condition of process itself as totality, without beginning or end, which is to say, as the experience of cultural immersion; the destruction of hierarchies and the *apparent* elimination of the culture of the elite in the post-colonial world; the internationalization of culture in what is now a global rather than local or even national context; and, in conclusion, the end of a culture of ordered self-reflection and so the beginning of a rapidly shifting, nonlinear culture of pure experience unhindered by rationality and doubt, a culture to be lived rather than reflected upon.[3] Again, all of these contestations, positive or negative, must be constantly *tested* within local, national, and international settings in order to determine their viability.

These considerations have implications for both cultural studies and for comparative literature, at least as practiced in the United States. The debates in Italy over these topics (and especially the "spin" that *il pensiero debole* put on them in the 1980's) were animated, to put it mildly, and often embittered by underlying sociopolitical motivations; these debates are now continuing in a more rigorous fashion in the pages of such recently established journals as *Allegoria* in Siena and *Avanguardia* in Rome (both of which, however, have editorial groups that usually regard postmodernism as a tendency or movement-based notion rather than as an epochal one). But these discussions have been more consistent and somewhat more profound on the American academic scene. When cultural studies began to gain a foothold in the academy in the United States, and especially in comparative literature programs in the early 1980's, it seemed to have the same sort of rejuvenating effect as did the importation of Marxist and structuralist theory in the late 1960's and early 1970's and of deconstruction in the mid-1970's. What literary theory did in a very positive and forceful way for comparative literature in that period seems to have been repeated by what cultural studies has done more recently, particularly regarding topics that previous approaches tended to treat either marginally (politics, social organization) or not at all (gender, technology). These topics have now come to the fore throughout critical studies. Regardless of the divisions within cultural studies today, as well as the ongoing divisions within comparative literature and literary theory, it appears important in conclusion to emphasize in this context the great lesson that Vico has taught us, that as social individuals, trained scholars, institutionally steeped academics, and whatever else we may be, we are first and foremost constructed subjects, but constructed *historically*, at once free *and* limited, and it is to that freedom, that limitation, and to the history and future of both, that we must now turn our collective focus.

REFERENCE MATTER

Notes

CHAPTER 1

1. See Fredric Jameson, *The Political Unconscious: Narrative as a Socially Symbolic Act* (Ithaca, N.Y.: Cornell University Press, 1981), and Myra Jehlen, *Class and Character in Faulkner's South* (New York: Columbia University Press, 1976). See also Jameson's *Postmodernism, or, The Cultural Logic of Late Capitalism*, Post-Contemporary Interventions (Durham, N.C.: Duke University Press, 1991).

2. In this regard, see Samuel Weber, *Institution and Interpretation*, Theory and History of Literature, no. 31 (Minneapolis: University of Minnesota Press, 1987).

3. See Fredric Jameson, *Marxism and Form: Twentieth-Century Dialectical Theories of Literature* (Princeton, N.J.: Princeton University Press, 1971), p. 375, and *The Ideologies of Theory: Essays 1971–1986*, 2 vols. Theory and History of Literature, nos. 48–49 (Minneapolis: University of Minnesota Press, 1988), 1:121; and Barbara Johnson, *A World of Difference* (Baltimore: Johns Hopkins University Press, 1987), p. 16.

4. Teresa de Lauretis, *Technologies of Gender: Essays on Theory, Film and Fiction*, Theories of Representation and Difference (Bloomington and Indianapolis: Indiana University Press, 1987).

5. See Judith Butler and Joan W. Scott, eds., *Feminists Theorize the Political* (New York and London: Routledge, 1992). Among the most germane essays here are those by Butler, Scott, Spivak, Haraway, Poovey, Chow, Schultz, Mouffe, Marcus, Alonso, and Singer. It is noteworthy that de Lauretis's own work is discussed at key moments throughout this anthology.

6. See Lucia Chiavola Birnbaum, *"Liberazione della donna": Feminism in Italy* (Middletown, Conn.: Washington University Press, 1986). The usefulness of this book is in part vitiated by Birnbaum's emphasis on Sicily (though it is also true that her focus on the South makes her work all the more interesting from an Italo-American viewpoint).

7. At the margins of the academy, Italian feminism has developed on its own in recent years by means of feminist groups in Italy's major cities, often, though not always, taking French feminist thought as their guiding model. On this topic see Judith Adler Hellman, *Journeys Among Women: Feminism in Five Italian Cities* (Cambridge: Polity Press, 1987) and Lucia Re, "Feminist Thought in Italy: Sexual Difference and the Question of Authority," *Michigan Romance Studies*, 16 (1996), pp. 61–86, in which Re focuses on the activities and the separatist intellectual tendencies of the Diotima group, a philosophical community of women begun in the University of Verona but moving beyond the university setting in various ways. In this regard see also the translation of the reader of the Milan Women's Bookstore Collective, *Sexual Difference: A Theory of Social-Symbolic Practice*, introductory essay by Teresa de Lauretis (Bloomington: Indiana University Press, 1990), and Rebecca West, "*Via Dogana*: A Journal By and For Women," in *The Literary Journal as a Cultural Witness, 1943–1993: Fifty Years of Italian and Italian American Reviews*, ed. Luigi Fontanella and Lucia Somigli, Filibrary, 10 (Stony Brook, N.Y.: *Forum Italicum*, 1966), pp. 149–60. Along with studies published in Italy, of related interest are the extremely useful collection of essays in *The Lonely Mirror: Italian Perspectives on Feminist Theory*, ed. Sandra Kemp and Paola Bono (London: Routledge, 1993) and the recent though distinctly uneven group of essays in *Italian Women Writers from the Renaissance to the Present: Revising the Canon*, ed. and introd. Maria Ornella Marotti (University Park: Pennsylvania State University Press, 1996). Yet the relative lack of success of feminism within the Italian academy, especially in humanistic studies, remains notable.

8. See, for example, Terry Eagleton, "Capitalism, Modernism and Post-modernism," in *Against the Grain: Essays 1975–1985* (London: Verso, 1986), pp. 131–47, and Eagleton, "From the *Polis* to Postmodernism," *The Ideology of the Aesthetic* (Oxford: Blackwell, 1990), pp. 366–417.

9. Gianni Vattimo, *La società trasparente* (Milan: Garzanti, 1989), p. 13; English cited from *The Transparent Society*, trans. David Webb (Baltimore: Johns Hopkins University Press, 1992), p. 5.

10. See Edward W. Said, "Traveling Theory," in *The World, the Text, and the Critic* (Cambridge, Mass.: Harvard University Press, 1983), pp. 226–47.

11. Jameson, *Political Unconscious*, p. 9.

CHAPTER 2

1. See for example the issue of *Critical Inquiry* devoted to the topic "Pluralism and Its Discontents," 12, no. 3 (Spring 1986), including essays by Wayne C. Booth, Hayden White, W. J. T. Mitchell, Ihab Hassan, Bruce Erlich, Ellen Rooney, Nelson Goodman and Catherine Z. Elgin, and Richard McKeon.

2. Ellen Frances Rooney, *Seductive Reasoning: Pluralism as the Problematic of Contemporary Literary Theory* (Ithaca, N.Y.: Cornell University Press, 1989), pp. 3, 2.

3. Wayne C. Booth, *Critical Understanding: The Powers and Limits of Pluralism* (Chicago: University of Chicago Press, 1979), p. 197.

4. Rooney, *Seductive Reasoning*, p. 5.

5. See Garry Wills, *Nixon Agonistes: The Crisis of the Self-Made Man* (Boston: Houghton Mifflin, 1970), and Louis Hartz, *The Liberal Tradition in America: An Interpretation of American Political Thought Since the Revolution* (New York: Harcourt, Brace and World, 1955). For a sensitive treatment of current American criticism in the light of the liberal tradition described by Hartz, see also Samuel Weber, "Capitalizing History: Notes on *The Political Unconscious*," *Diacritics*, 13, no. 2 (Summer 1983): 14–28, revised in *Institution and Interpretation* (Minneapolis: University of Minnesota Press, 1987), pp. 40–58.

6. Booth, *Critical Understanding*. Booth's major interlocutors over the course of this study are Ronald Crane, Kenneth Burke, and M. H. Abrams.

7. See especially R. S. Crane, *The Languages of Criticism and the Structure of Poetry*, The Alexander Lectures (Toronto: University of Toronto Press, 1953); Richard McKeon, *Thought, Action and Passion* (Chicago: University of Chicago Press, 1954); and Elder Olson, "The Dialectical Foundations of Critical Pluralism" (1966), reprinted in *"On Value Judgments in the Arts" and Other Essays* (Chicago: University of Chicago Press, 1976), pp. 327–59. Of somewhat lesser import in this context, see Wayne C. Booth, *The Rhetoric of Fiction* (Chicago: University of Chicago Press, 1961), with its dedication to Crane and its homage to McKeon's pluralist influence (p. 403), and Sheldon Sacks, *Fiction and the Shape of Belief: A Study of Henry Fielding. With Glances at Swift, Johnson and Richardson* (Berkeley: University of California Press, 1964). See also Booth's *The Company We Keep: An Ethics of Fiction* (Berkeley: University of California Press, 1988).

8. William James, *A Pluralistic Universe*, ed. Fredson Bowers and Ignas K. Skrupskelis, introd. Richard J. Bernstein, The Works of William James (Cambridge, Mass.: Harvard University Press, 1977). For Booth's comments, see *Critical Understanding*, pp. 73–74.

9. James, *Pluralistic Universe*, p. 9.

10. Ibid. p. 149; Booth, *Critical Understanding*, p. 197.

11. Hugh Kenner, *A Homemade World: The American Modernist Writers* (Knopf; reprint, New York: William Morrow, 1975).

12. Wayne C. Booth, " 'Preserving the Exemplar': Or, How Not to Dig Our Own Graves," *Critical Inquiry*, 3, no. 3 (Spring 1977): 420. This forum was a part of the debate over the nature and limits of pluralism that began with J. Hillis Miller's review of M. H. Abrams's *Natural Supernaturalism: Tradition and Revolution in Romantic Literature* (New York: Norton, 1971); see Miller, "Tradition and Difference," *Diacritics*, 2, no. 4 (Winter 1972): 6–13. See also Booth, "M. H. Abrams: Historian as Critic, Critic as Pluralist," *Critical Inquiry*, 2, no. 3 (Spring 1976): 411–45; M. H. Abrams, "Rationality and Imagination in Cultural History: A Reply to Wayne Booth," *Critical Inquiry*, 2, no. 3 (Spring 1976): 447–64; Abrams, "The Deconstructive Angel," *Critical Inquiry*, 3, no. 3 (Spring 1977); 425–38; Abrams, "Behaviorism and Deconstruction: A Comment on Morse Peckham's 'The Infinitude of Pluralism,' " *Critical Inquiry*, 4, no. 1 (Autumn 1977): 181–93; Abrams, "How to Do Things with Texts," *Partisan Review*, 46, no. 4 (1979): 566–88; and Miller, "The Critic as Host," *Critical Inquiry*, 3, no. 3 (Spring 1977): 439–47. For a recent, distinctly nonpluralist assessment of the issues at stake in these discussions, see Tobin Siebers, "Language, Violence, and the Sacred: A Polemical Survey of Critical Theories," *Stanford French Review* ("To Honor René Girard"), 10, nos. 1–3 (1986): 203–19.

13. Booth, "Preserving the Exemplar," p. 422, my italics.

14. Ibid., p. 423.

15. Stanley Fish, *Is There a Text in This Class? The Authority of Interpretive Communities* (Cambridge, Mass.: Harvard University Press, 1980), p. 299. Fish's positions, while expanded, remain principally unchanged in his *Doing What Comes Naturally: Change, Rhetoric, and the Practice of Theory in Literary and Legal Studies*, Post-Contemporary Interventions (Durham, N.C.: Duke University Press, 1989).

16. Fish, *Is There a Text in This Class?*, p. 321.

17. Ibid., p. 355. For a discussion of Fish's use of the terminology of agonistic combat and of his habit of delimiting the borders of debate in order to stay within those borders (and, therefore, not to entertain the broader social and political implications of his arguments), see Samuel Weber, *Institution and Interpretation*, pp. 33–58. Weber (following Louis Hartz) sees the sort of tactics that Fish adopts as characteristic of the American liberal community cut off from its roots in European history, and Weber extends his argument to include the institutional framework within which contemporary critics operate, that is, the departments of literary studies in American universities.

18. See E. D. Hirsch, Jr., *Validity in Interpretation* (New Haven, Conn.: Yale University Press, 1967). See also Hirsch, *The Aims of Interpretation* (Chicago: University of Chicago Press, 1976), especially pp. 1–13.

19. Hirsch, *Validity in Interpretation*, p. 164, my italics.

20. Ibid., p. 139.

21. E. D. Hirsch, Jr., "Coming with Terms to Meaning," *Critical Inquiry*, 12, no. 3 (Spring 1986): 630.

22. See Fredric Jameson, *The Political Unconscious: Narrative as a Socially Symbolic Act* (Ithaca, N.Y.: Cornell University Press, 1981), pp. 9, 14, 17, 19, et passim.

23. See Samuel Weber, "Capitalizing History," and Ellen Rooney, *Seductive Reasoning*, chap. 6. For White's elaboration on his praise for Jameson's syncretist tendencies, see Hayden White, "Getting Out of History: Jameson's Redemption of Narrative" (1982), revised version in *The Content of the Form: Narrative Discourse and Historical Representation* (Baltimore: Johns Hopkins University Press, 1987), pp. 142–68.

24. Paul B. Armstrong, "The Conflict of Interpretations and the Limits of Pluralism," *PMLA*, 98, no. 3 (May 1983): 341–52. Armstrong's three criteria for the validity of any reading (which, as I have mentioned, remain thoroughly within the pluralist problematic) involve inclusiveness, intersubjectivity, and efficacy. Armstrong discusses these and related topics at greater length in his study *Conflicting Readings: Variety and Validity in Interpretation* (Chapel Hill: University of North Carolina Press, 1990).

25. See David Tracy, *Blessed Rage for Order: The New Pluralism in Theology* (New York: Seabury Press, 1975); *The Analogical Imagination: Christian Theology and the Culture of Pluralism* (New York: Crossroad, 1981); and *Plurality and Ambiguity: Hermeneutics, Religion, Hope* (New York: Harper and Row, 1987). Interestingly enough, Tracy has regularly taught a course at Chicago on the multiple foundations of ethics together with Paul Ricoeur.

26. Wayne C. Booth, *Modern Dogma and the Rhetoric of Assent*, University of Notre Dame Ward-Phillips Lectures in English Language and Literature, no. 5 (Notre Dame, Ind.: University of Notre Dame Press, 1974).

27. These meetings were held on the University of Michigan campus in Ann Arbor. For an example of Said's earlier work, see *Beginnings: Intention and Method* (Baltimore: Johns Hopkins University Press, 1975). Among his more recent works, see *Orientalism* (New York: Random House, 1978) and *The World, the Text, and the Critic* (Cambridge, Mass.: Harvard University Press, 1983), especially "Traveling Theory," pp. 226–47, in which Said mentions the specifically "Goethean sense of a concert of all literatures and ideas" (p. 228).

28. Derrida's interview with James Kearn and Ken Newton, *Literary Review* 14 (Apr.–May 1980), p. 21, is cited by Ellen Rooney at the open-

ing of her essay "Who's Left Out? A Rose by Any Other Name Is Still Red; Or, The Politics of Pluralism," *Critical Inquiry*, 12, no. 3 (Spring 1980): 550–63, and in *Seductive Reasoning*, pp. 19, 239.

29. Gianni Vattimo, *La fine della modernità*, Saggi blu (Milan: Garzanti, 1985); translated by Jon R. Snyder as *The End of Modernity: Nihilism and Hermeneutics in Postmodern Culture*, Parallax: Re-visions of Culture and Society (London: Polity; Baltimore: Johns Hopkins University Press, 1988), which includes an extraordinarily convincing and precise introduction to Vattimo's thought by the translator (pp. vi–lviii).

30. In the last two chapters and the conclusion of my *Beautiful Fables: Self-consciousness in Italian Narrative from Manzoni to Calvino* (Baltimore: Johns Hopkins University Press, 1986), I discuss (although not in direct relation to Vattimo's work) the possibility that postmodern self-consciousness differs from modernist self-consciousness precisely in not allowing for authoritative critical closure on the part of the author, the text itself, or the reader.

CHAPTER 3

1. On the New York group of Marxist intellectuals in the 1930's, see especially Alan M. Wald, *The New York Intellectuals: The Rise and Decline of the Anti-Stalinist Left from the 1930s to the 1980s* (Chapel Hill: University of North Carolina Press, 1987). The most germane of Fredric Jameson's works in this context are *Marxism and Form: Twentieth-Century Dialectical Theories of Literature* (Princeton, N.J.: Princeton University Press, 1971); *The Political Unconscious: Narrative as a Socially Symbolic Act* (Ithaca, N.Y.: Cornell University Press, 1981); and *The Ideologies of Theory: Essays 1971–1986*, 2 vols. (Minneapolis: University of Minnesota Press, 1988).

2. Jameson, *Marxism and Form*, p. ix.

3. For treatment of the singular importance of Trotsky's thought for the *Partisan Review* group in the late 1930's (including discussion of Trotsky's correspondence with them, preserved in the Houghton Library of Harvard University and recently opened to the public), see Marlene Kadar, "Partisan Culture in the Thirties: *Partisan Review*, the Surrealists and Leon Trotsky," *Canadian Review of Comparative Literature*, 13, no. 3 (Sept. 1986): 375–423. See also Wald, *New York Intellectuals*, chap. 5.

4. Stanley Aronowitz suggests this comparison, with a keen awareness of its ironies, in *The Crisis in Historical Materialism: Class, Politics and Culture in Marxist Theory*, A J. F. Bergin Publishers Book (New York: Praeger, 1981), p. 248. Aronowitz cites in particular Trilling's *The Liberal Imagination* (New York: Viking, 1950) as Trilling's rediscovery of the

value of the subjective imagination as opposed to the supposedly communal objectivism of socialist realism.

On the development of Marxist thought in regard to the New York journals of the 1930's (including the extremely complicated and often confusing interrelations of the various editorial and political groups in question), see James Burkhart Gilbert, *Writers and Partisans: A History of Literary Radicalism in America*, American Cultural History Series (New York: John Wiley and Sons, 1968), especially chaps. 3–6.

5. Wald, *New York Intellectuals*, p. 46 *passim.*

6. Among these, see Wilson's revaluation of the empiricist and materialist strains of modern historiography, beginning with Vico and ending with Lenin, in Edmund Wilson, *To the Finland Station: A Study in the Writing and Acting of History* (Garden City, N.Y.: Doubleday, 1940); and Matthiessen's historical (though avowedly non-Marxist) approach, deriving from such historically oriented American critical forebears as Van Wyck Brooks and Vernon Parrington, first in F. O. Matthiessen, *American Renaissance: Art and Experience in the Age of Emerson and Whitman* (New York: Oxford University Press, 1941), and then in his "The Responsibilities of the Critic" (1949), in which Matthiessen insists on "the primacy of economic factors in society," in *The Responsibilities of the Critic: Essays and Reviews by F. O. Matthiessen*, ed. John Rackliffe (New York: Oxford University Press, 1952), pp. 3–18, quotation from p. 10.

7. See Granville Hicks, *The Great Tradition: An Interpretation of American Literature Since the Civil War* (New York: Macmillan, 1933/1935), pp. 301–6.

8. Rahv, writing in 1950, states, "In the 1930's the key term was 'revolution' while now it is 'tradition.'" Philip Rahv, "Religion and the Intellectuals," in *Essays in Literature and Politics: 1932–1972*, ed. Arabel J. Porter and Andrew J. Duosin (Boston: Houghton Mifflin, 1978), p. 310. In this same collection (p. 304), see also Rahv's polemical remarks (from 1939) on Hicks's *Great Tradition*. For Macdonald's later views on his own position in the 1930's (including a perspective on the 1950's and beyond), see his *Memoirs of a Revolutionist: Essays in Political Criticism* (New York: Farrar, Strauss and Cudahy, 1957), especially p. 4: "The difference then and now in the New York intellectual atmosphere—in this context New York is America as Paris is France—is that then we believed in revolution and now we don't." It should be noted that from a strictly traditional Marxist viewpoint the genuineness of the "revolutionary" perspective of these writers, even in the 1930's, has been questioned: see Lawrence H. Schwartz, *Marxism and Culture: The CPUSA and Aesthetics in the 1930's*, National University Publications Literary Criticism Series (Port Washington, N.Y.: Kennikat Press, 1980), p. 68 et passim. Although

such questioning is always possible, I think that in this instance Schwartz overstates his case.

9. See Jameson, "Periodizing the 6os," in *Ideologies of Theory*, 2: 178–208.

10. Wald, *New York Intellectuals*, pp. 3–24.

11. In Neil Larson's foreword to volume 1 of Jameson's *Ideologies of Theory*, Larson comments on the odd amalgam of European and American traditions at work in Jameson's writing, and he also notes Terry Eagleton's and Samuel Weber's remarks in a similar vein, in "Capitalizing History," *Institution and Interpretation* (Minneapolis: University of Minnesota Press, 1987), pp. 40–58.

12. Regarding Jameson's view of literature as a reflection of class struggle, see especially *Marxism and Form*'s lengthy closing essay, "Towards Dialectical Criticism," pp. 306–416.

13. Jameson, *Political Unconscious*, p. 76.

14. Jameson, *Ideologies of Theory*, 2: viii–ix, a passage perhaps evincing a Foucauldian echo.

15. See Fredric Jameson, *Postmodernism; or, The Cultural Logic of Late Capitalism* (Durham, N.C.: Duke University Press, 1991).

16. See "Fredric Jameson sul postmoderno. Nota crtica di Gregory Lucente," *Avanguardia* 1, no. 1 (1996): 6–9, in which I treat Jameson's usual reflection schema in terms of his addition of consistent critical "uncertainty" to his previous understanding of the postmodern, thus opening up postmodernism, at least in potential, to a more positive reading.

17. See Richard Ohmann, *English in America: A Radical View of the Profession* (New York and London: Oxford University Press, 1976); and Michael Ryan, *Marxism and Deconstruction: A Critical Articulation* (Baltimore and London: Johns Hopkins University Press, 1982).

18. See Jack J. Roth, "The 'Revolution of the Mind': The Politics of Surrealism Reconsidered," *South Atlantic Quarterly*, 72, no. 2 (1977): 147–58, in which Roth describes the differences in the concept of revolution between the French surrealists (especially Breton), Trotsky, and the leaders of the French Communist Party.

19. See Jameson, *Political Unconscious*, p. 102; Jameson, *Ideologies of Theory*, 2: 73–74; Aronowitz, *Crisis in Historical Materialism*, pp. xi–xix.

20. See especially Aronowitz, *Crisis in Historical Materialism*, p. xxiii; Jameson, *Ideologies of Theory*, 1: 110, 2: 37–60, 73–74, 174–208.

21. See Jameson, *Ideologies of Theory*, 1: 167 and 2: 48–49.

22. Bertell Ollman and Edward Vernoff, eds., *The Left Academy: Marxist Scholarship on American Campuses* (New York: McGraw-Hill, 1982).

23. See Edward Said, "Reflections on American 'Left' Literary Criticism," in *The World, the Text, and the Critic* (Cambridge, Mass.: Harvard University Press, 1983), pp. 158–77.

24. This point is made in various contexts in the course of Samuel Weber's *Institution and Interpretation*.

25. See Jameson, "Architecture and the Critique of Ideology," in *Ideologies of Theory*, 2: 35–60.

CHAPTER 4

This essay was researched and written in collaboration with Gloria Lauri Lucente.

1. Joseph Buttigieg is currently at work on a complete translation of Gramsci's *Prison Notebooks* (New York: Columbia University Press), which, when published in its totality, will resolve at least a few of the problems addressed in this essay.

2. Antonio Gramsci, "Introduzione alla filosofia" (1932–33), in *Quaderni del carcere*, Edizione critica dell'Istituto Gramsci, 4 vols., ed. Valentino Gerratana (Turin: Einaudi, 1975), 2: 1379–80 (Quaderno 11 [xviii], 1932–33); and Antonio Gramsci, *Selections from the Prison Notebooks*, ed. and trans. Quinton Hoare and Geoffrey Nowell Smith (New York: International, 1971), p. 327.

3. Gramsci, quoted from the Hoare and Smith translation in *Selections*, in Edward Said, "Reflections on American 'Left' Literary Criticism," in Said's *The World, the Text, and the Critic* (Cambridge, Mass.: Harvard University Press, 1983), p. 170. Although the translation by Quinton Hoare and Geoffrey Smith is throughout extraordinarily accurate word for word, it is also true that it is accurate *only* word for word. They assigned themselves not only the task of translating but also that of editing, and while their *translation* is careful, they have *edited* Gramsci in a fashion that would have made Bowdler proud by omitting, modifying, and knitting together sections of the *Quaderni* into a whole that reduces over three thousand pages of text and notes to roughly five hundred pages in translation, that repeatedly softens the impact of Gramsci's polemics, that hides the specificity of his historical and philosophical reference, and that renders his thought — as well as subsequent reference to that thought — next to impossible to trace in his actual writings. Following this caveat, I should note that Said's use of Gramsci in this instance does not in any way reflect the problems of this selection in translation.

4. Said, "Reflections," pp. 170–71.

5. See "Conclusion: Vico in His Work and in This," in Edward Said, *Beginnings: Intention and Method* (Baltimore: Johns Hopkins University Press, 1975), pp. 345–81.

6. See Gayatri Spivak, "Subaltern Studies: Deconstructing Historiography," in her *In Other Worlds: Essays in Cultural Politics* (New York: Routledge, 1988), pp. 19–221; and Gayatri Spivak, "Can the Subaltern

Speak?," in *Marxism and the Interpretation of Culture*, ed. and intro. Cary Nelson and Lawrence Grossberg (Urbana: University of Illinois Press, 1983), pp. 271–313.

7. Spivak, "Deconstructing Historiography," p. 198.

8. Ibid. The superscript in parentheses indicates a superscript in the original text.

9. Nelson and Grossberg, preface to *Marxism and the Interpretation of Culture*, p. ix, my italics.

10. Antonio Gramsci, "Some Aspects of the Southern Question," in his *Selections from Political Writings (1921–1926)*, ed. and trans. Quinton Hoare (1978; reprint, Minneapolis: University of Minnesota Press, 1990), pp. 441–62.

11. The following extract is cited from Spivak, "Can the Subaltern Speak?," p. 283. The superscript in parentheses at the end indicates a superscript in the original text.

12. See, for example, de Man's foreword to Carol Jacobs's *The Dissimulating Harmony: The Image of Interpretation in Nietzsche, Rilke, Artaud, and Benjamin* (Baltimore: Johns Hopkins University Press, 1978), and his 1978 preface to his special edition of the journal *Studies in Romanticism*.

13. Paul de Man, *Allegories of Reading: Figural Language in Rousseau, Nietzsche, Rilke, and Proust* (New Haven, Conn.: Yale University Press, 1979), p. ix.

14. In the series of interviews in Edward Said, *The Pen and the Sword: Conversations with David Barsamian*, intro. Eqbal Ahmad (Monroe, Me.: Common Courage Press, 1994), it is completely clear from occasional remarks how deeply Said has thought about Gramsci's work, though always from Said's own particular perspective (see especially pp. 93, 142). This is also true in Said's recently published Reith Lecturers, most notably at the beginning and at the inspired and, to my mind, totally convincing conclusion regarding intellectuals and social action: *Representations of the Intellectual: The 1993 Reith Lectures* (New York: Pantheon Books, 1994). See also the Gramscian arguments in Said's *Culture and Imperialism* (New York: Random House/Vintage, 1993), which includes a version of Said's round-table talk "Connecting Empire to Secular Interpretation" (pp. 43–61), to which I refer in Chapter 2 of this study. All of this work demonstrates Said's profound understanding of and commitment to the *overall* tendencies of Gramsci's thought.

15. Stanley Aronowitz, *The Crisis in Historical Materialism: Class, Politics and Culture in Marxist Theory*, A J. F. Bergin Publishers Book (New York: Praeger, 1981); and Aronowitz, "Postmodernism and Politics," in *Universal Abandon? The Politics of Postmodernism*, ed. Andrew Ross (Minneapolis: University of Minnesota Press, 1988), pp. 46–62.

16. For Tony Bennett's doubts on this point, see his "Putting Policy into Cultural Studies," in *Cultural Studies*, ed. and intro. Lawrence Grossberg, Cary Nelson, and Paula A. Treichler (New York: Routledge, 1992), pp. 23–33.

17. Stuart Hall, "Theoretical Legacies," in Grossberg, Nelson, and Treichler, *Cultural Studies*, p. 286. Hall's paper was originally addressed to an academic conference on cultural studies held at the University of Illinois, Urbana-Champaign, in April 1990. The exchanges following Hall's talk (pp. 286–94) are also of interest. They cover issues ranging from the development of cultural studies in English to the role of intellectuals in society, the value of theory, problems of professional hierarchy and exclusion, and the dangers of the academic "success" and consequent institutionalization of cultural studies in the United States.

18. See her reference to Gramsci and the question of the formation of intellectuals in Gayatri Spivak, *Outside in the Teaching Machine* (New York: Routledge, 1993), p. 244.

CHAPTER 5

1. All references are to the 1744 edition of Giambattista Vico, *Scienza nuova*, in *Opere*, ed. Fausto Nicolini, vol. 4, tomes 1–2, Scrittori d'Italia, nos. 112–13 (Bari: Laterza, 1928). Translations are from *The New Science of Giambattista Vico: Unabridged Translation of the Third Edition (1744)*, trans. Thomas Goddard Bergin and Max Harold Fisch, rev. ed. (Ithaca, N.Y.: Cornell University Press, 1968), which, on occasion, I have altered slightly for accuracy. Paragraph numbers, identical for original and translation, are included in the text.

2. B. A. Haddock, *Vico's Political Thought* (Swansea: Mortlake Press, 1986), p. 194. Haddock, whose treatment of the issue is singularly rigorous and evenhanded, goes on to insist on the specifically Christian aspect of the system that Vico uses as his model. Haddock also includes a brief but useful bibliography of the deeply contrasting positions on this vexed question (p. 228 n.174).

3. See Gregory Lucente, "Vico's Notion of 'Divine Providence' and the Limits of Human Knowledge, Freedom, and Will," *MLN*, 97 (1982): 183–91.

4. From a somewhat different historical perspective, Giuseppe Mazzotta treats Vico's adoption of an encyclopedic form in which, via the examination of etymologies, Vico provides criticism of both Baconian empiricism and Cartesian rationalism within Vico's own characteristic mix of reason and imagination, intellectual curiosity and wonder. See Mazzotta's "Vico's Encyclopedia," *Yale Journal of Criticism*, 1, no. 2: 65–79.

CHAPTER 6

1. For a critical overview of the evidence of this impact see Giorgio Tagliacozzo's three-part essay, "Toward a History of Recent Anglo-American Vico Scholarship" ("Part I: 1944–1969" *New Vico Studies*, 1 [1983]: 1–20, especially p. 12; "Part II: 1969–1973," *New Vico Studies*, 2 [1984]: 1–40, especially pp. 26–26, 36–40; "Part III: 1974–1977," *New Vico Studies*, 3 [1985]: 1–32, especially pp. 11–14, 22–23). This material, along with major additions, has now appeared as part of Tagliacozzo's study, *The "Arbor Scientiae" Reconceived and the History of Vico's Resurrection* (Atlantic Highlands, N.J.: Humanities Press International, 1993).

2. Hayden White, *The Content of the Form: Narrative Discourse and Historical Representation* (Baltimore: Johns Hopkins University Press, 1987).

3. Jorge Luis Borges, "The Fearful Sphere of Pascal," in his *Labyrinths: Selected Stories and Other Writings*, ed. Donald A. Yates and James E. Irby (New York: New Directions, 1964), p. 192.

4. Hayden White, "Vico and the Radical Wing of Structuralist/Poststructuralist Thought Today," *New Vico Studies*, 1 (1983): 63–68.

5. For a discussion of both Pompa's position and White's treatment of it (which appeared in White's review in *History and Theory*, 15 [1976]: 186–202), see Tagliacozzo, "Toward a History of Recent Anglo-American Vico Scholarship," *New Vico Studies*, 3 (1985): 11–14.

6. See, for example, Peter de Bolla's incisive discussion of White's recent work in "Disfiguring History," *Diacritics*, 16, no. 4 (Winter 1986): 49–58, and Stephen Bann's briefer treatment, "Hayden White and History," *London Review of Books*, Sept. 17, 1987, pp. 17–18. For White's interest in narrative as discursive metaphor, see especially *The Content of the Form*, pp. 91, 156–57.

7. White, *The Content of the Form*, p. 168.

CHAPTER 7

1. All references to Gramsci's notebooks are to Antonio Gramsci, *Quaderni del carcere*, Edizione critica dell'Istituto Gramsci, ed. Valentino Gerratana, 4 vols. (Turin: Einaudi, 1975). One of the few precise acknowledgments of the importance of Gramsci's notion of reciprocity is found in Alberto Gramese's study, *Parco centrale: Critica letteraria e sociologia della produzione culturale*, Riscontri, no. 8 (Naples: Fratelli Conte, 1979), especially chaps. 1–2.

2. Gramsci, *Quaderni del carcere*, 3: 1822.

3. Ibid., 3: 1677, 1821, 2122, 2195.

4. Alberto Asor Rosa, *Scrittori e popolo: Il populismo nella letteratura italiana contemporanea* (Rome: Savelli, 1965). Asor Rosa reaffirms the substance of his original position, while taking a somewhat more dialectical tone, in his new introduction ("Vent'anni dopo") to Einaudi's reprint of *Scrittori e popolo*, Gli struzzi, no. 337 (Turin: Einaudi, 1988), pp. vii–xviii.

5. *Gramsci e la cultura contemporanea: Atti del convegno internazionale di studi gramsciani tenuto a Cagliari il 23–27 aprile 1967*, 2 vols. (Rome: Editori Riuniti/Instituto Gramsci, 1969–70).

6. See Norberto Bobbio, "Gramsci e la concezione della società civile," in *Gramsci e la cultura contemporanea*, 1: 75–100.

7. See Natalino Sapegno, "Gramsci e i problemi della letteratura," in *Gramsci e la cultura contemporanea*, 1: 265–77.

8. See Carlo Salinari, "La struttura ideologica dei 'Promessi sposi,'" and response by Edoardo Sanguineti, "Glosse a Salinari," both in *Critica marxista* 12, nos. 3–4 (1974): 183–200, 201–6. A longer version of Salinari's essay, which also served as the introduction to his edition of the novel, appeared in the posthumously published collection of his critical pieces, *Boccaccio Manzoni Pirandello*, ed. Nino Borsellino and Enrico Ghidetti, intro. Natalino Sapegno, Nuova biblioteca di cultura, no. 193 (Rome: Riuniti, 1979), pp. 113–57.

9. In Sebastiano Timpanaro, "Antileopardiani e neomoderati nella sinistra italiana," *Belfagor*, 30, nos. 2, 4; 31, nos. 1, 2 (1975–76), reprinted in *Antileopardiani e neomoderati nella sinistra italiana* (Pisa: ETS, 1982).

10. See Alberto Cirese, "Concezioni del mondo, filosofia spontanea, folclore," in *Gramsci e la cultura contemporanea*, 2: 299–328.

11. Collected in Furio Diaz et al., *Egemonia e democrazia: Gramsci e le questione comunista nel dibattito di Mondoperaio*, intro. Federico Coen, Quaderni di Mondoperaio, no. 7 (Rome: Edizioni Avanti!, 1977). Also of some interest in this period was the conference on Gramsci's thought held in Florence in December 1977, published as *Politica e storia in Gramsci: Atti del convegno internazionale di studi gramsciani*, ed. Franco Ferri, Nuova biblioteca di cultura, no. 202 (Rome: Editori Riuniti/Istituto Gramsci, 1979).

12. Important documents regarding Gramsci are already coming to light. In this context see *L'ultima ricerca di Paolo Spriano: Dagli archivi dell'URSS i documenti segreti sui tentativi per salvare Antonio Gramsci* (Rome: L'Unità, 1988). The content of the documents located in the Soviet archives seems to be confirmed by Giulio Andreotti's findings in the corresponding archives in the Vatican (in which regard see *Il tempo*, Oct. 30, 1988).

CHAPTER 8

1. References to Pirandello's works are to the following editions: *Maschere nude*, vol. 5 of *Opere di Luigi Pirandello*, I classici contemporanei italiani (Milan: Mondadori, 1958/1968); *Saggi, poesie, scritti varii*, ed. Manlio Lo Vecchio-Musti, vol. 6 of *Opere di Luigi Pirandello*, I classici contemporanei italiani (Milan: Mondadori, 1939/1960); *Tutti i romanzi*, 2 vols., ed. Giovanni Macchia and Mario Costanzo, *Opere di Luigi Pirandello*, I Meridiani (Milan: Mondadori, 1973). Translations of the Italian are mine throughout.

2. See Gregory Lucente, " 'Non conclude': Self-Consciousness and the Boundaries of Modernism in Pirandello's Narrative," *Criticism*, 26 (1984): 21–47; revised version printed in *Beautiful Fables: Self-consciousness in Italian Narrative from Manzoni to Calvino* (Baltimore: Johns Hopkins University Press, 1986), pp. 116–55.

3. Luigi Pirandello, *L'umorismo*, in *Saggi*, pp. 15–160.

4. Luigi Pirandello, *Uno, nessuno e centomila*, in *Tutti i romanzi*, p. 901.

5. Luigi Pirandello, *Lazzaro*, in *Maschere nude*, p. 1218; cf. p. 1216.

6. *Naked Masks: Five Plays by Luigi Pirandello* ed. Eric Bentley (New York: Dutton, 1952).

7. The opening pages of the novel were published for the first time in Pirandello, *Saggi*, pp. 1057–59.

8. Pirandello's commentary is found in an explanatory note accompanying "I fantasmi" (an early section of *I giganti della montagna*), published in *Nuova Antologia*, 280, no. 7 (Dec. 1931): 475–99.

9. Luigi Pirandello, *I giganti della montagna*, in *Maschere nude*, p. 1346.

10. Ibid.

11. Marta Abba's argument, which suffers from an obvious (though understandable) personal bias, is set forth in the preface and the concluding note to her edition of *I giganti della montagna*, Teatro di tutti i tempi, no. 9 (Milan: Mursia, 1966/1972), pp. 5–11, 135–40.

12. Pirandello, *I giganti della montagna*, p. 1336.

13. Ibid., p. 1307.

14. Ibid., p. 1362, my italics.

15. For Marta Abba's confession of her own displeasure with *I giganti* at first hearing Pirandello's reading of it, see her edition, p. 135.

CHAPTER 9

1. All references are to Elsa Morante, *La Storia*, Gli struzzi, 58 (Turin: Einaudi, 1974); translated by William Weaver as *History: A Novel* (New York: Knopf, 1977).

2. Gregory Lucente, "*Scrivere o fare . . . o altro:* Social Commitment and Ideologies of Representation in the Debates over Lampedusa's *Il Gattopardo* and Morante's *La Storia,*" *Italica,* 61, no. 3 (Sept. 1984): 220–51.

3. Morante, *La Storia,* pp. 646–49; *History,* pp. 546–48.

4. Cf. Morante, *La Storia,* pp. 29, 69; *History,* pp. 25, 59.

5. Published as Elsa Morante, "La censura in Spagna," *L'unitá,* May 15, 1976, and Elsa Morante, " 'La Storia' secondo Elsa Morante," *Corriere della sera,* May 15, 1976. Translations are mine.

6. See Roberto González Echevarría, "*Cien Años de Soledad:* The Novel as Myth and Archive," *MLN,* 99, no. 2 (1984): 358–80, reprinted in *Myth and Archive: A Theory of Latin American Narrative* (Cambridge, Eng.: Cambridge University Press, 1990); Sara Castro-Klarén, "Locura y dolor: La elaboración de la historia en *Os Sertões* y *La guerra del fin del mundo,*" *Revista de Critica Literaria Latinoamericana,* no. 20 (1985): 207–31, and Castro-Klarén, "Santos and Cangaceiros: Inscription Without Discourse in *Os Sertões* and *La guerra del fin del mundo,*" *MLN,* 101, no. 2 (1986): 366–88.

CHAPTER 10

1. Antonio Gramsci, *Quaderni del carcere,* Edizione critica dell'Istituto gramsci, ed. Valentino Gerratana, 4 vols. (Turin: Einaudi, 1975), 2: 1210.

2. See Jacques Derrida, "Like the Sound of the Sea Deep Within a Shell: Paul de Man's War," *Critical Inquiry,* 14, no. 3 (1988): 590–652.

3. On this issue see especially Derrida, "Like the Sound," pp. 591–92 et passim; Mark Edmundson, "A Will to Cultural Power: Deconstructing the de Man Scandal," *Harper's,* 227 (July 1988): 67–71; and J. Hillis Miller, "Two Current Debates," *Times Literary Supplement,* June 17–23, 1988, pp. 676, 685. In his article, which is paired with a thoughtful essay by Tzvetan Todorov, Miller laments not only the lack of previous interest in and experience with literary theory on the part of journalists in the United States but also the virulent attack on deconstruction and theory as a whole spawned by the de Man revelations.

4. Paul de Man, *Wartime Journalism, 1939–1943,* ed. Werner Hamacher, Neil Hertz, and Thomas Keenan (Lincoln: University of Nebraska Press, 1988), and by the same editors, *Responses: On Paul de Man's Wartime Journalism* (Lincoln: University of Nebraska Press, 1989). Originally all of this material was to be published by the *Oxford Review,* but it became too bulky for them to manage.

5. Richard Klein first suggested the importance that the elder de Man had for the younger (though initially taking Hendrik for Paul de Man's father) in "The Blindness of Hyperboles: The Ellipses of Insight," *Diacrit-*

ics, 3, no. 2 (Summer 1973): 33–44. See also Derrida, "Like the Sound," pp. 604–6 n. 12. James Atlas claims that at times de Man himself actively contributed to the confusion between uncle and father, in "The Case of Paul de Man," *New York Times Magazine*, Aug. 28, 1988, p. 60.

6. Geoffrey Hartman, "Blindness and Insight: Paul de Man, Fascism, and Deconstruction," *The New Republic*, Mar. 7, 1988, p. 26.

7. Derrida, "Like the Sound," p. 631.

8. Paul de Man, "Les Juifs dans la littérature actuelle," *Le Soir*, Mar. 4, 1941, p. 10, and Paul de Man, "Paul Valéry et la poésie symboliste," *Le Soir*, Jan. 10–11, 1942, p. 3.

9. This is not to lessen the import of the anti-Semitic cast of de Man's comments. It is perhaps worthy of note that a schematic version of these same opinions—along with a somewhat mitigated portrayal of the role of the Jews in modern literature, specifically the German novel—recurs in an article by de Man ("Blik op de huidige Duitsche romanliteratuur," p. 2), published in Flemish in *Het Vlaamsche Land* on August 20, 1942, that is, just over two weeks after the first train of Belgian Jews left for Auschwitz.

10. De Man's critique of totalities, including historical as well as logical and phenomenological ones, extended even to his assessment of the pseudo-unity of his own works and those of his colleagues as collected and published in book form. See, for three among various possible examples, his prefaces to his books *Allegories of Reading: Figural Language in Rousseau, Nietzsche, Rilke, and Proust* (New Haven, Conn.: Yale University Press, 1979), pp. ix–xi, and *The Rhetoric of Romanticism* (New York: Columbia University Press, 1984), pp. vii–ix, and his foreword to Carol Jacobs's *The Dissimulating Harmony: The Image of Interpretation in Nietzsche, Rilke, Artaud, and Benjamin* (Baltimore: Johns Hopkins University Press, 1978), pp. vii–xiii. This foreword is now collected in de Man's *Critical Writings, 1953–1978*, ed. Lindsay Waters, Theory and History of Literature, 66 (Minneapolis: University of Minnesota Press, 1989), pp. 218–23.

11. Hartman, "Blindness and Insight," p. 26.

12. Derrida, "Like the Sound," pp. 647–49, 652.

13. Ibid., p. 591.

14. Ibid., pp. 592–93, my italics.

15. David Lehman, "Deconstructing de Man's Life: An Academic Idol Falls into Disgrace," *Newsweek*, Feb. 15, 1988.

CHAPTER 11

1. *Against Theory: Literary Studies and the New Pragmatism*, ed. W. J. T. Mitchell (Chicago: University of Chicago Press, 1985).

2. See Steven Knapp and Walter Benn Michaels, "Against Theory," in *Against Theory*, pp. 11–30; and Knapp and Michaels, "Against Theory 2: Hermeneutics and Deconstruction," *Critical Inquiry* 14, no. 1 (1987): 49–68. Page references to these two essays and to the Mitchell volume will be included in my text, accompanied by the following abbreviations: AT for "Against Theory," AT2 for "Against Theory 2," and *AT* for *Against Theory*.

3. The term is Laurence Lerner's, in a review of *Against Theory* in *Comparative Literature*, 40, no. 1 (1988): 69.

4. Peggy Kamuf, "Floating Authorship," *Diacritics*, 16, no. 3 (1986): 3–13.

5. See Jacques Derrida, "Signature Event Context" and "Limited Inc abc . . . ," and John Searle, "Reiterating the Differences: A Reply to Derrida," all in *Glyph*, 1–2 (1977).

6. Kamuf was not alone in her doubts: see E. D. Hirsch, "Against Theory?," in *AT*, pp. 50–51, and Richard Rorty, "Philosophy Without Principles," in *AT*, p. 137 n. 6.

7. Steven Knapp and Walter Benn Michaels, "A Reply to Our Critics," in *AT*, p. 103. On this point see Hirsch, "Against Theory?," pp. 51–52.

8. Knapp and Michaels use P. D. Juhl's *Interpretation: An Essay in the Philosophy of Literary Criticism* (Princeton, N.J.: Princeton University Press, 1980) to extend their treatment of Hirsch's intentionalist argument to include consideration of language and speech acts.

9. W. K. Wimsatt, Jr., and Monroe C. Beardsley, "The Intentional Fallacy," in *The Verbal Icon: Studies in the Meaning of Poetry* (Lexington: University of Kentucky Press, 1954), pp. 3–18.

10. Stanley Fish, *Is There a Text in This Class? The Authority of Interpretive Communities* (Cambridge, Mass.: Harvard University Press, 1980). Also see Fish's *Doing What Comes Naturally: Change, Rhetoric, and the Practice of Theory in Literary and Legal Studies*, Post-Contemporary Interventions (Durham: Duke University Press, 1989).

11. Kamuf, "Floating Authorship," p. 10.

12. Samuel Weber, *Institution and Interpretation*, Theory and History of Literature, no. 31 (Minneapolis: University of Minnesota Press, 1987), pp. 40–41.

13. See *AT*, pp. 107, 115, and 123.

CHAPTER 12

1. See Gianni Vattimo, *La fine della modernità*, Saggi blu (Milan: Garzanti, 1985), translated by Jon R. Snyder as *The End of Modernity: Nihilism and Hermeneutics in Postmodern Culture*, Parallax: Re-visions

of Culture and Society (London: Polity; Baltimore: Johns Hopkins University Press, 1988). Interestingly enough, it was precisely the chapter dealing with the "philosophy" of postmodernity (chap. 10, pp. 164–81) that was revised by Vattimo for this translation; the English version is, however, only slightly more convincing than the original.

2. See David Hayman, *Ulysses: The Mechanics of Meaning* (1970; reprint, Madison: University of Wisconsin Press, 1982).

3. Two recent though very different Italian novelists, Paolo Volponi and Maria Corti, have managed to incorporate allegorical critiques of social and symbolic systems into the postmodern novel, thus providing within the postmodern itself a renewed sense of hierarchical perspective. See Paolo Volponi, *Le mosche del capitale* (Turin: Einaudi, 1988), and Maria Corti, *Il canto delle sirene* (Milan: Bompiani, 1989). In Volponi's case, these hierarchies are not just social but also pointedly political.

Index

In this index, "f" after a page number indicates a separate reference on the next page; "ff" indicates separate references on the next two pages. A continuous discussion over two or more pages is indicated by a span of page numbers (e.g., "57–59"); *passim* is used for a cluster of references in close but not consecutive sequence.

Library of Congress Cataloging-in-Publication Data

Lucente, Gregory L.
    Crosspaths in literary theory and criticism : Italy
and the United States / Gregory L. Lucente.
            p.   cm.
    Includes bibliographical references and index.
    ISBN 0-8047-2829-1 (cloth: alk. paper). —
    ISBN 0-8047-2830-5 (pbk. alk. paper)
    1. Criticism.   2. Criticism — Italy.
    3. Criticism — United States.   I. Title.
    PN81.L83   1997
    801'.95'0945 — dc21   96-44321
                                                      CIP

⊗ This book is printed on acid-free, recycled paper.

Original printing 1997
Last figure below indicates year of this printing:
06 05 04 03 02 01 00 99 98 97